American Elegance

A WINTERTHUR BOOK

American Elegance

CLASSIC AND CONTEMPORARY

MENUS FROM CELEBRATED

HOSTS AND HOSTESSES

ABBEVILLE PRESS
PUBLISHERS NEW YORK

COMPILED BY
CHERYL K. GIBBS
WRITTEN BY
LUCINDA COSTIN
PHOTOGRAPHY BY
WINTERTHUR MUSEUM AND GARDENS
WITH A FOREWORD BY
BROOKE ASTOR

EDITOR: Alan Axelrod

DESIGNER: Nai Y. Chang

PRODUCTION SUPERVISOR: Hope Koturo

Copyright 1988 Winterthur Museum and Gardens

Published in the United States of America in 1988 by
Abbeville Press, Inc.

Printed and bound in Japan

LIBRARY OF CONGRESS
Library of Congress Cataloging-in-Publication Data

American elegance : classic and contemporary menus from
celebrated hosts and hostesses / compiled by Cheryl K. Gibbs :
written by Lucinda Costin ; photography by Winterthur
Museum and Gardens ; with a foreword by Brooke Astor.
p.   cm. — (A Winterthur book)
Includes index.
ISBN 0-89659-886-1
1. Cookery, American.   2. Menus.   3. Entertaining.   I. Gibbs,
Cheryl K. II. Costin, Lucinda.
TX715.A448 1988
641.5973—dc 19

Contents

Foreword

WINTERTHUR HOSPITALITY

When I married Charles Henry Marshall, I became the sister-in-law of Mrs. Marshall Field. She was an intimate friend of Henry Francis (Harry) and Ruth du Pont, and so, happily, I was drawn into their circle. Evie Field and the du Ponts were avid bridge players and played every day of their lives, and, on looking back, I wonder why they were so very kind to me because I did not play bridge. Perhaps it was because I admired them both so enormously and was full of curiosity about all of the interesting things that they did. I was quite a bit younger, and, in a way, they treated me almost as a daughter. I can never forget that when my husband Charles Marshall (Buddie) died suddenly, Harry and Ruth came up to visit me in the Tyringham Valley where we were living, bringing with them a roast turkey, a roast ham, a basket of peaches, and a huge basket of vegetables. When I exclaimed over their generosity and kindness, they simply said, "We always do this when we visit our children."

But, as I started to say, we (Buddie and I) were drawn into their circle because of Evie Field. We spent many weekends at Winterthur together, and I went often after Buddie's death.

From the very first, I was fascinated by the way that Harry du Pont ran the household. Ruth, who had a marvelous sense of humor, was not interested in house-keeping; however, she was a wonderful foil for Harry, and this made a flawless combination. She joked about his perfectionism while at the same time was very proud of this side of his character. He kept a list of guests and table settings, as he did not want to risk the chance of one duplication. There was no detail that escaped his eye.

He allowed me to go with him to his china closet once when I had stayed over Monday morning, and I was privileged to watch him choose the table decorations for the following weekend. The china closet was enormous, and its shelves were crowded with huge services of Spode, Crown Derby, Lowestoft, Worcester, Wedgwood, and so on. A footman climbed up on a ladder and gingerly brought down a few of the magnificent centerpieces that Harry had pointed out. Emil, the major-domo, and Harry indicated where they were to be placed on the large table in the center of the pantry for better viewing. Once the pieces were placed, the head gardener and the greenhouse man came in, bringing with them samples of flowers that would be in bloom over the weekend. This was done so that flowers and china service would complement each other. The whole process took an entire morning, as six or seven meals would have to be served from Friday night to Monday, and the

decorations for each were carefully written down. I had once asked Harry, before witnessing this procedure, if I could see a beautiful turquoise-and-silver Lowestoft service on the table during the weekend, and he had told me that it had not been planned. But he was extremely kind and took endless trouble to explain things when I asked such questions.

He also did very special things for the cocktail hour, such as serving caviar in a way that other servers of the exotic black eggs might like to follow. Small tables were set up temporarily outside the drawing room or in the hall, and formal place cards were placed at each seat so that you could have the fun of talking to two different people during the evening and not sit down casually next to your future dinner partner. The caviar was on ice in a huge glass bowl with dishes of grated egg whites and crisp slices of toast around it, and iced vodka was at each place beside a small plate with a knife and napkin. One could enjoy the delicious treat comfortably and to the full, which one cannot do standing up with a plate in one hand and a glass in the other.

Another delicacy that Winterthur was famous for was its marvelous terrapin, usually served at least once during the weekend. Terrapin has disappeared from menus; thus I am glad I enjoyed it so much at Winterthur.

Harry knew everything concerning botany and dendrology. His knowledge was endless, yet he never showed any sign of arrogance. He always answered me carefully by telling me the name, variety, and origin of a specimen as though I had asked him a most interesting and absorbing question. I remember his saying once that he had started his azalea garden with only seventeen azaleas and had propagated all the rest of the huge collection at Winterthur, crossing many varieties to achieve extraordinary colors. He was never without a notebook in his hand and wrote down everything, noting every flower, bush, and tree that he thought needed pruning or care.

Looking back, I realize more than ever how wonderful it was to have seen Winterthur in all its beauty and how fortunate I was to have been there as a guest and to have enjoyed the warmth and hospitality of the du Ponts. As I have said, Ruth and Harry were wonderful complements to each other. He was an aesthete and she was down-to-earth. As a reflection of her great sense of humor, Ruth wrote the most amusing verse with which she would regale us.

All in all, it was a great experience. Perhaps I should add that later on, just before they moved into their new home on the estate, Harry was good enough to let me come down as feature editor of *House and Garden* with a great bevy of photographers to photograph Winterthur. This was another one of his kindnesses.

June 1987   BROOKE ASTOR

The Duncan Phyfe-style mahogany card table, ca. 1805, made in New York, is in perfect harmony with the mahogany lyre-back side chairs, ca. 1810. Gilded guilloche leaf bands decorate the Chinese porcelain, ca. 1790. Early nineteenth-century knives with silver repoussé handles add a glow to the eighteenth-century glasses and cut-glass decanter.

Introduction

ENTERTAINING IN THE WINTERTHUR STYLE

Like the Xanadu of Orson Welles's *Citizen Kane*, Winterthur is an immense mansion —some two hundred rooms—set in a vast domain—over nine hundred acres—and stocked with an extraordinary array of rare and beautiful objects—more than 70,000 of them. But unlike the fictional and omnivorous Charles Foster Kane, the real-life Henry Francis du Pont acquired his fabulous collection lovingly and with great discrimination. Where life at Xanadu was massive and graceless, days and evenings at Winterthur—tremendous as it was and is—consisted of graceful and gracious attention to detail. And this was as evident in the way the du Ponts entertained as it was in the collection Henry Francis so joyfully acquired.

Mr. du Pont, who began collecting in the early 1920s, expanded the Winterthur house to three times its original size in order to accommodate his collection of decorative art objects made or used in America before 1840. By the time he founded the museum in 1951, he had amassed more than fifty thousand pieces, including porcelain dinnerware and vases, crystal decanters and drinking glasses, silver flatware and candle holders, and antique linens. These provided him with more than enough of everything he needed to set an elegant table.

But you need not have unlimited resources of food, flowers, and fine antiques in order to entertain elegantly. You need only pay attention to detail, take care in food preparation and presentation, and exercise imagination.

Entertaining in the Winterthur style means creating a relaxed, memorable meal, filled with pleasure, fine food, and friends. While the Winterthur style was established many years ago, in an era more leisurely than our own, it lives again in menus devised by prominent connoisseurs, collectors, and patrons of the arts. We know that you and your guests will find great pleasure in them.

Elegance has been the hallmark of entertaining at Winterthur for generations. Henry Francis du Pont, the founder of Winterthur Museum, loved to entertain, often

---

Yuletide at Winterthur is an annual event. The Marlboro Room is ready for an eighteenth-century dinner for family, friends, and neighbors. Small tables are placed in the largest room to accommodate the gathering. A "Great Pie" with an elaborate pastry cover was served during the first course of the meal.

PHOTO REPRINTED FROM *Recreating Yuletides Past* © 1987

hosting as many as forty guests for a weekend's festivities. His daughters, Pauline du Pont Harrison and Ruth du Pont Lord, remember "guests at every meal, with laughter and lively conversation."

Great attention was given the menu for each meal, with Mr. and Mrs. du Pont, their head chef, and their butler collaborating to serve interesting and delicious fare. According to the du Pont daughters, the table always looked beautiful, whether set for breakfast, lunch, or dinner.

Each meal was highlighted by the use of antique china, crystal, linens, and flatware, often juxtaposed with contemporary pieces. Flowers were also featured at every meal, whether as single buds or extravagant displays. And always Mr. du Pont alone chose the table settings, drawing on his vast knowledge of and love for American antiques and horticulture. He used his antiques to create special settings for his guests to enjoy, and his table settings, like his room arrangements, were carefully designed and meticulously carried out, becoming an environment for a meal rather than just a backdrop for it.

Glassware at Winterthur included virtually every type used in early America. Pieces of engraved, cut, and enameled glassware were part of the collection. Wineglasses with bowls of bell, funnel, trumpet, thistle, or flute shape; cordial glasses and rummers; tumblers and ale glasses; and firing glasses—those sturdy manufactured glasses that sound like gun shots when they are touched together in a toast-all —had an assigned purpose at the du Pont table. Decanters were used for storing and serving the wine that accompanied dinner every evening.

Each meal required several plates, as Mr. du Pont chose to follow the French custom of serving separate courses. Chinese export porcelain made for the European and American markets; French, Dutch, and English porcelain and ceramics, some depicting American or Oriental scenes; and even early American porcelain were used at meal times. A favorite, and rare, dessert service tells of entertaining in the eighteenth century. Six plates bear these verses:

What is a Merry Man
Let him do What he Can
To Entertain his Guests
With Wine & Merry Jests
But if his Wife do Frown
All Merriment Goes Down

Under Henry Francis du Pont, the Winterthur estate reached its great size, with almost two thousand acres of cultivated land and pasture. The working farm was virtually self-sufficient, having herds of beef and dairy cattle, sheep, pigs, flocks of chickens, turkeys, guinea hens, terrapin (kept in the cellar), ducks, squab, fruit and nut orchards, and hothouses and outdoor gardens for flowers and vegetables. Mr. du Pont's passion for horticulture and farming provided ample resources for his dinner table. The freshest foods and flowers were a notable part of entertaining at Winterthur.

Mr. du Pont was known for grouping flowers of one variety in an arrangement, with several vases of the same flower placed around the table. Often single blooms or small vases of flowers were used; large opulent arrangements were reserved for formal dinner tables.

At other times, flowers of assorted colors and types were displayed. When roses were in bloom, blossoms of red, yellow, pink, white, magenta, coral, and pale orange might all be in the same vase. Spring flowers were often mixed, with profuse arrangements of daffodils, tulips, early irises, and flowering branches celebrating the abundance of the season.

Some table settings were designed around a particular flower. A notable meal at Winterthur was a dinner to mark the opening of a fragile, night-blooming "cigar plant." An exotic setting that mixed antique Chinese porcelain, modern bamboo flatware, and rattan candle holders complemented the unique blossoms. Closed at the beginning of dinner, the flowers made a dramatic entrance—opening to reveal vibrant pink featherlike petals, their color picked up in the pale pink linens on the table.

Lunch was invariably a formal meal at Winterthur, beginning with an egg dish and including a vegetable, meat, salad, and dessert. Dinner was even more elegant, with soup, fish, meat, two vegetables, salad, cheese, and dessert served. Holiday meals for the du Pont family required special arrangements. The Christmas holiday was always an important time at Winterthur, a time for family and traditions. This

Winterthur's "Merryman" plates, ca. 1717, are one of the few series of tin-glazed earthenware plates still in existence.

spirit is remembered in the museum's annual tour, "Yuletide at Winterthur," which celebrates the holiday customs of early America. Christmas meals were often limited to the immediate du Pont family and very close friends. While it was not uncommon to see thirty at dinner on a Saturday evening, Christmas dinner rarely included more than twelve guests.

Christmas settings did not change from year to year. Both Mrs. Harrison and Mrs. Lord recall a special glass regularly placed on the Christmas dinner table for sherry to season the annual terrapin stew. Luncheon featured white English porcelain bordered with a delicate green vine. Green-tinted glassware, pale green placemats, and elegant arrangements of white Roman hyacinths and paperwhite narcissus complemented the dishes. The family favored a red-and-gold color scheme at Christmas dinner, laying the table with a transfer-printed dinner set, gold goblets, and a crisp white tablecloth.

Whether for a holiday or for "everyday," entertaining was a necessary component of a full and enjoyable life at Winterthur. Family members looked forward to house parties with great enthusiasm. The success of these gatherings must also have stemmed from the sure knowledge of the guests that their company was appreciated and enjoyed by their hosts.

Sampling of porcelain patterns dating from the early eighteenth century to the mid nineteenth century.

Conveying a similar appreciation and enjoyment is the most important ingredient for successful entertaining in any setting. Beyond this, it is also crucial that you carefully plan both the menu and the table setting. A formal dinner party is not the best occasion for experimenting with new dishes. Stay with the familiar. Make as much of the meal as possible ahead of time, and set the table well before the guests are to arrive. Being prepared eases tension before the meal and allows you to enjoy your assembled company.

If you are seating guests rather than having them seat themselves, pay careful attention to the arrangement. Although guests with like interests may be seated together, placing guests next to each other who have dissimilar but compatible interests can lead to lively conversation.

One area that does lend itself to experimentation at any time is the table setting. The most interesting tables are frequently those that combine antiques and modern dishware. Ornate antique porcelain and streamlined, modern glassware can look quite wonderful together. Slick monotone dinnerware can be the perfect complement to an elaborate lace tablecloth. The dinnerware need not match; a different plate at each place can solve the problem of how to serve a large number of people without benefit of a large dinner service. Using dishes with different patterns for hors d'oeuvres, dinner, and dessert is also acceptable and often more stimulating than using dishes with a single pattern throughout the meal. Having several small tables, each with a different dinner service, flower arrangement, and color for table linens, is another way to provide an intimate dining experience for a large group of guests. Even furniture need not match. But be sure not to have too much variety in the table arrangements! At Winterthur, large gatherings often meant that a variety of chairs —painted, plain, ladder back, curved back, rush seated, and carved—were used to accommodate the many guests. Find a common denominator in the furnishings (a particular color, height, or type) and then provide variations on the theme.

Flowers are important to any elegant meal. Whether presented as a single bloom, an overblown arrangement, or several arrangements, flowers add grace and festivity to any lunch or dinner table. Select flowers that will not detract from the experience of the meal. Avoid heavily scented blossoms and large arrangements that obstruct a diner's view of his companions. Also, the flowers should carry out the mood suggested by the menu. Spiky, exotic arrangements may be perfect for a multicourse Chinese dinner, but they are inappropriate at a Victorian-style afternoon tea.

A meal need not be served in a formal dining room to be memorable. A cheery country kitchen is the best place for a hearty winter breakfast. A tree-shaded terrace has no match as the setting for a late-night summer dinner. Whether the guests arrive in a horse-drawn carriage or in the basket of a hot-air balloon, a picnic has a special place in the hearts of most people. Seafood can taste no better than when it is steamed in a pit and served to guests gathered on a beach as night falls.

The key is creativity.

CHAPTER ONE

Breakfast and Brunches

A COUNTRY BREAKFAST FROM WINTERTHUR MUSEUM

Long before Winterthur was a world-renowned museum of American decorative arts, it was a working estate with dairy and beef cattle, sheep, turkeys, fruit and nut orchards, vegetable and flower gardens, and a saw mill. The self-sufficient Winterthur Farm enjoyed its heyday under the direction of Henry Francis du Pont, when its property incorporated close to two thousand acres. Such a profitable enterprise owed its success to many people, including the families who lived on the estate and worked its land.

A hearty farm breakfast was the norm at Winterthur, as evidenced by this meal garnered from the Winterthur Archives. Before a long day of hard work, a meal including Country Sausage Patties, Cinnamon Apple and Bran Waffles, Hot Cider Sauce, and fresh fruit juice might be served. Naturally, as many of the ingredients as possible came directly from the Winterthur estate.

A country kitchen welcomes breakfasters to this filling—and fueling—meal, which is as delicious today as it was earlier in the century. A fire lies ready to give warmth on a brisk autumn morning, before the day's chores begin. The colorful

This cozy New England kitchen, part of the Winterthur Museum, is based on the kitchen of a house in Oxford, Massachusetts, ca. 1740. The red-painted pine-and-birch table and the Windsor chairs are characteristic New England pieces from this period. The Pennsylvania earthenware plates, dating from the eighteenth and early nineteenth centuries, have unique spidery floral motifs in "sgraffito," a technique in which a design is scratched through the "slip"—a fluid ceramic glaze—to reveal the body color beneath before the earthenware is fired in the kiln. The early nineteenth-century basswood butter mold, also Pennsylvanian, displays the familiar sheaf-of-wheat motif. The steel forks, ca. 1834, with floral-inlay bone handles, were made by John Russell and Company of Massachusetts. The knives, ca. 1830, also steel, have horn handles and were made by J. A. Ashmore of Philadelphia.

earthenware dishes and pitchers hold food, drink, and sauces, brightening a chilly morning when the family must be up before the sun. Napkins are wrapped in colorful rings of bittersweet, a sure sign of fall. And extra fruit is placed as a centerpiece, as "dessert" for *really* hungry family members.

Serve steaming-hot coffee and tea with the meal, as well as a variety of fresh-squeezed juices. If desired, be adventurous and serve orange-pineapple or grapefruit-banana juice instead of the usual favorites.

Menu

Fresh Fruit

Country Sausage Patties

Fresh Cinnamon Apple Waffles

Tasty Bran Waffles

Hot Cider Sauce

Milk—Coffee—Tea

Juice

PREPARATION TIPS: WAFFLES

Deservedly, waffles are a breakfast favorite. Hot from the waffle iron, covered with butter, syrup, jam, or fresh fruit, they are always a sunny way to start the day. Although they are relatively easy to prepare, they do take some time—for heating the waffle iron or letting the batter sit—so they are often passed over for quicker pancakes, French toast, or even frozen "toaster" waffles. Prepare waffles for a Sunday brunch. The reviews are sure to be raves!

A few things to keep in mind: first, waffles are cooked when the waffle iron stops steaming. Do not open the waffle iron before then, as the waffles may stick to it and break. If the iron does not open easily once steam has stopped, let the waffle cook for a few more seconds.

For easier removal of waffles, the iron may be brushed with butter or a light coating of vegetable oil. If the iron is very hot and lightly greased, sticking should not be a problem.

Try several kinds of waffles. Waffles can be varied by adding fruit, chopped nuts, or herbs and spices to the batter. They can also be served topped with various kinds of syrups and jams, sliced fresh fruit, breakfast meats, or even creamed chipped beef or scrambled eggs. Also, try waffles instead of biscuits or breads at lunch and dinner.

COUNTRY SAUSAGE PATTIES

Number of Servings: 10

Preparation Time: 30 minutes

Cooking Time: 30 minutes

INGREDIENTS:

 1 ½ cups rolled oats
 ¾ cup water
 1 ¼ pounds lean pork tenderloin, partially frozen
 ½ pound veal, partially frozen
 1 pound fresh pork fat, partially frozen
 3 ice cubes
 2 teaspoons salt
 ⅛ teaspoon ground allspice
 ⅛ teaspoon ginger
 ⅛ teaspoon sage

DIRECTIONS:

Bring oats and water to a boil in a small saucepan, then drain immediately and cool in refrigerator for 15 minutes.

Cut pork, veal, and pork fat into 1-inch pieces; coarsely chop in food processor, two or three handfuls of meat and fat and 1 ice cube at a time. Combine meats, fat, oats, and seasonings, kneading or working the mixture thoroughly with your fingers.

Shape into patties. Refrigerate or cook immediately.

FRESH CINNAMON APPLE WAFFLES

Number of Servings: 4–5 large

Preparation Time: 15 minutes

Cooking Time: 20 minutes

INGREDIENTS:

1¾ cups all-purpose flour, sifted
1 tablespoon sugar
1 teaspoon cinnamon
2½ teaspoons baking powder
½ teaspoon salt
2 egg yolks, beaten
1¼ cups milk
2 tablespoons vegetable oil
2 apples, peeled, cored, and finely chopped
2 egg whites, stiff-beaten

DIRECTIONS:

Sift together first 5 ingredients. Combine egg yolks, milk, and vegetable oil. Add to dry ingredients; mix well. Stir in apples. Fold in egg whites. Bake in preheated waffle iron.

TASTY BRAN WAFFLES

Number of Servings: 4–5 large

Preparation Time: 15 minutes

Cooking Time: 20 minutes

INGREDIENTS:

1 cup sifted all-purpose flour
¼ cup sugar
1 teaspoon baking powder
½ teaspoon baking soda
¼ teaspoon salt
1 cup buttermilk
2 egg yolks, beaten
1 cup whole bran cereal
½ cup raisins, chopped
6 tablespoons butter or margarine, melted
2 egg whites, stiff-beaten

DIRECTIONS:

Sift together first 5 ingredients in mixing bowl. Stir in buttermilk and beaten egg yolks. Stir in cereal, raisins, and melted butter. Fold in beaten egg whites. Bake in preheated waffle iron.

HOT CIDER SAUCE

Yield: 2 cups

Preparation Time: 5 minutes

Cooking Time: 15 minutes

INGREDIENTS:

2 cups brown sugar
2 cups apple cider
2 tablespoons butter or margarine
1 teaspoon lemon juice
½ teaspoon ground cinnamon
¼ teaspoon ground nutmeg

DIRECTIONS:

In saucepan, combine brown sugar, cider, butter, lemon juice, cinnamon, and nutmeg. Bring mixture to a boil; simmer 15 minutes, or until sauce is slightly thickened. Serve hot.

A SPRING BRUNCH FROM *BON APPÉTIT*

Spring is the loveliest season at Winterthur. Henry Francis du Pont planned his lavish, naturalized gardens to reach their full glory at this time of year. Continuous color is evident in the gardens from the bloom of the first crocus in March to the display of the last vibrant rhododendron in late June.

What better time than spring to have a leisurely weekend brunch in Winterthur's gardens? And what better source than *Bon Appétit* for a brunch befitting Winterthur's stature? For chefs worldwide the magazine sets standards in culinary art, just as Winterthur sets standards in decorative arts.

This *Bon Appétit* menu provides unique breakfast ideas; some of the dishes can be prepared ahead to save brunch-day hassles. Individual Breakfast Strudels are a savory treat sure to pique even the laziest weekend appetite. They are an innovative change from traditional sausage and eggs and can be prepared a day in advance.

Canadian Bacon with Apricot Glaze provides a blend of sweet and savory flavors, as does the Salad of bittersweet Watercress and Mushrooms. Piping-hot Lemon-Date Muffins, made with honey and sour cream, round out this flavorful meal.

Serve this weekend brunch with a sweet hot tea, such as English breakfast or orange pekoe, and Bloody Marys.

Menu

Salad of Watercress and Mushrooms

Individual Breakfast Strudels

Pan-Fried Canadian Bacon with Apricot Glaze

Steamed Asparagus with Butter ‡

Lemon-Date Muffins

Tea

Bloody Marys

The Winterthur reproduction fabric "Abigail" by Albert Van Luit & Company is beautiful as a table covering. Its design was taken from an English wood-block-printed cotton, ca. 1808. The cloth accents the white glazed plates at each setting, which were made in Staffordshire, England, ca. 1750–1780. The creamy white salt-glazed teapot, ca: 1745, was probably made by Thomas and John Wedgwood. It is slip cast in the form of a rectangular three-story house complete with double-arch entrances framing a standing figure. Mottahedeh reproduction creamware cups and saucers complete the place settings. A crystal pear and apple at the table's center are echoed in the fruit-shaped glass napkin rings.

PREPARATION TIP: MUFFINS

Muffins are easy to make if a few simple rules are followed. First, "less is more." Mix the dry and liquid ingredients until a thick, lumpy batter forms. Then spoon the batter into lined or greased muffin tins and bake immediately. Overmixed muffins tend to be dry and heavy.

Second, be exact. As in all baking, the finished product is better if ingredients are properly measured. Also, the texture, density, and appearance of muffins will be better if they are cooked at the correct heat. A too hot or too cold oven will cook muffins unevenly, leaving them coarse and unattractive.

Sour cream is used in this recipe for the moistness and the slightly tart flavor that it imparts to the muffins. For a low-fat alternative, try using plain yogurt.

SALAD OF WATERCRESS AND MUSHROOMS

Number of Servings: 6

Preparation Time: 5 minutes, plus 30 minutes to marinate

INGREDIENTS:

¼ cup balsamic vinegar
½ teaspoon salt
½ teaspoon (scant) Dijon mustard
¾ cup olive oil
¾ pound mushrooms, quartered
1½ cups watercress leaves

DIRECTIONS:

Mix vinegar, salt, and mustard in large bowl. Gradually whisk in oil in a thin stream. Stir in mushrooms. Let marinate for 30 minutes, stirring occasionally. Just before serving, add watercress to salad and toss to coat with dressing.

✠

INDIVIDUAL BREAKFAST STRUDELS

Number of Servings: 6

Preparation Time: 35 minutes

Cooking Time: 15 minutes

INGREDIENTS:

1½ tablespoons butter
1½ tablespoons all-purpose flour
¾ cup milk
6 tablespoons (2½ ounces) Gruyère cheese, grated
2 tablespoons Parmesan cheese, freshly grated
¼ teaspoon salt
Pinch of cayenne pepper
Fresh ground nutmeg
¼ pound bulk pork sausage
5 eggs
1½ teaspoons fresh, minced thyme
¼ teaspoon salt
Fresh ground pepper
1 tablespoon butter
1 tablespoon fresh parsley, minced
6 phyllo pastry sheets
½ cup (1 stick) unsalted butter, melted
6 tablespoons dry bread crumbs
Fresh thyme sprigs

DIRECTIONS:

Melt 1½ tablespoons butter in heavy medium saucepan over medium-low heat. Add flour and stir 3 minutes. Gradually whisk in milk. Continue whisking until mixture thickens and comes to a boil. Remove from heat. Stir in cheeses, 4 tablespoons at a time. Add salt and pinch of cayenne pepper. Season generously with nutmeg. Pour into medium bowl.

Cook sausage in heavy medium skillet over medium-high heat until no longer pink, breaking up with fork. Mix eggs, minced thyme, salt, and pepper in medium bowl. Add sausage, using slotted spoon. Heat 1 tablespoon butter in heavy large skillet over high heat. Add eggs to sausage mixture and stir with fork until just set but still moist. Mix into cheese sauce. Add parsley. Adjust seasoning. Cool completely.

Butter rimmed baking sheet. Arrange 1 phyllo pastry sheet on towel on work surface (keep remaining pastry sheets covered with a damp towel). Generously brush pastry with melted butter. Sprinkle with 1 tablespoon of the bread crumbs. Fold sheet in half lengthwise. Brush surface with butter. Spoon ⅓ cup of egg and sausage filling along a short end of the pastry sheet. Spread the mixture 3 inches down the length of the pastry, leaving ¾-inch border on the edges. Fold edges of pastry over filling.

Starting at short end with filling, fold dough up to form package. Arrange seam side down on prepared baking sheet. Brush top with butter. Repeat with remaining pastry sheets. (Can be prepared 1 day ahead to this point. Wrap in plastic and refrigerate. On the day to be served, let stand at room temperature while oven is preheating.)

Position rack in center of oven and preheat oven to 375 degrees. Bake strudels until golden brown, about 15 minutes. Cool 5 minutes before serving. Garnish each strudel with fresh thyme sprigs.

PAN-FRIED CANADIAN BACON WITH APRICOT GLAZE

Number of Servings: 6

Preparation Time: 10 minutes

Cooking Time: 8 minutes

INGREDIENTS:

½ cup apricot preserves
2 teaspoons Dijon mustard
2 teaspoons hoisin sauce (available at oriental markets)
2 tablespoons (¼ stick) butter
10 ounces Canadian bacon, cut into ⅛-inch-thick slices

DIRECTIONS:

Combine apricot preserves, mustard, and hoisin sauce in heavy small skillet over medium heat. Stir until preserves melt. Strain through fine sieve.

Melt butter in heavy large skillet over medium-high heat. Add bacon (in batches if necessary) and cook until light brown, turning occasionally, about 4 minutes. Transfer to platter. Brush top generously with glaze. Serve bacon immediately.

LEMON-DATE MUFFINS

Yield: 14 muffins

Preparation Time: 15 minutes

Cooking Time: 20 minutes

INGREDIENTS:

½ cup light brown sugar, firmly packed
6 tablespoons (¾ stick) unsalted butter
5 tablespoons fresh lemon juice
¼ cup honey
½ cup sour cream
1 egg
1 tablespoon lemon peel, grated
1¾ cups all-purpose flour
1½ teaspoons baking powder
¾ teaspoon salt
½ teaspoon baking soda
1 cup dates, chopped
⅔ cup pecans, coarsely chopped
¼ cup hot water

DIRECTIONS:

Preheat oven to 400 degrees. Generously butter 14 2½-inch muffin cups. Cook brown sugar, butter, lemon juice, and honey in heavy medium saucepan over medium heat until hot, stirring constantly. Cool slightly.

Whisk sour cream, egg, and lemon peel in medium bowl to blend. Add warm brown sugar mixture. Combine flour, baking powder, salt, and baking soda in another bowl. Add to liquid ingredients and stir until just blended. Add dates, pecans, and hot water and mix 10 seconds; mixture will be lumpy. Fill prepared muffin cups two-thirds full with batter. Bake until muffins are puffed and golden brown, about 20 minutes. Serve hot or warm. To reheat muffins bake in a 300-degree oven for about 5 minutes.

BRUNCH WITH THE BUNCH

On "The Cosby Show" and in daily life, the role of father is a familiar and funny one for Bill Cosby. As on television, where he oversees the Huxtable clan, Mr. Cosby in real life rules a roost of five children. But the multifaceted Bill Cosby is more than just America's favorite father.

As a comedian, in his top-rated television show and best-selling books and videos, Mr. Cosby is a chronicler of the uniqueness of the American family and American life. As a collector of Afro-American art, Shaker furniture, and early American decorative arts, Mr. Cosby is also a chronicler of American culture and history.

Any meal with Bill Cosby is bound to be an all-American family affair, and Brunch with the Bunch is no exception. A menu highlighted by Bill's special sauce provides a hearty way to start the day, important for runners like Mr. Cosby or for those who prefer to be spectators. Side dishes of Red Beans and Rice round out the meal.

A colorful, casual table setting is a must for the relaxed weekend get-together. Here, the table is highlighted by spatterware dishes complemented by homespun linens and fresh flowers from the garden.

Serve this brunch with piping hot coffee, freshly brewed tea, and plenty of fresh-squeezed orange juice. Keep some sparkling water on hand to use as a mixer for a light, refreshing change.

Menu

Fresh Orange Juice

Honeydew Wedges with Lemon ‡

Poached Eggs and Sausage with Bill's Special Sauce

Red Beans

Rice ‡

Corn Bread

Fresh Whole Wheat Bread ‡

English Breakfast Tea

Coffee

---

‡ (recipes not included)

PREPARATION TIPS:

Corn bread, red beans, and tea were the mainstay of the American diet during the nation's early years. Most recipes took hours to prepare. Corn bread was at least a half-day process: first crushing the corn, then blending the corn meal with water and forming the mixture into cakes, and finally cooking the cakes over an open fire or in the ashes. The bean pot was kept on a slow fire in the fireplace for the entire day. It required tending every few hours to make sure there was enough water in the pot. Once the beans were cooked, they were kept ready to be served for several meals.

Modern conveniences, such as microwave ovens, pressure cookers, and crock pots, make preparing time-consuming recipes a breeze. There is no need to be afraid of these new conveniences; simply follow the manufacturer's instructions. Soon you will find yourself preparing dishes that usually take hours in a matter of minutes. These new fast methods of cooking also retain the vitamins and minerals in food, giving you a more nutritious meal.

The rare communal dining table made of cherry, maple, and pine is from the Shaker community of New Lebanon, New York, ca. 1800. The painted comb-back Windsor armchairs originated in New England and Pennsylvania, ca. 1760–1810. Both chairs have long tapered spindles and a narrow, U-shaped arm rail that widens at the front. The dinnerware is called spatterware, an eighteenth-century English ware from Staffordshire, which is spattered with a brush or sponge. Reserves were normally left in the center ground to contain painted motifs such as the distelfink—a stylized Pennsylvania German bird motif— shown. The English cutlery set, ca. 1790, is made of steel, silver, and bone. All the knife blades are stamped "SAVORY & PRYOR"; all the forks have two tines. Modern stemware complements the colorful table setting.

BILL'S SPECIAL SAUCE

Number of Servings: 16

Preparation Time: 15 minutes, plus overnight for marinating

Cooking Time: 25 minutes

INGREDIENTS:

2 cups sliced onions
½ cup extra virgin olive oil
Tons of fresh minced garlic
2 tablespoons thyme, chopped
2 tablespoons oregano
2 bay leaves
2 pounds beautiful, fresh, ripe tomatoes, peeled, seeded, chopped
2 cups dry white wine
1 6-ounce can tomato paste
1 pound button mushrooms
1 pound wild mushrooms (portobella, morels, shiitake, oyster)
2 pints pitted black olives
2 tablespoons chopped basil
2 teaspoons anchovy paste
Fresh ground pepper
2 cups sun-dried tomatoes (soaked in vinegar overnight and drained, marinated in olive oil and basil)

DIRECTIONS:

Sauté onions in olive oil until they are transparent. Add garlic, chopped thyme, oregano, and bay leaves. Sauté for one minute. Add tomatoes, white wine, and tomato paste. Simmer 10 minutes. Slice button mushrooms and wild mushrooms. Add sliced mushrooms and olives. Reduce over low heat until thick.

Just before serving, add chopped basil, anchovy paste, fresh ground pepper, and drained sun-dried tomatoes. Simmer about 5 minutes and serve.

Also perfect on spaghetti.

✥

CORN BREAD

Yield: 18 muffins

Preparation Time: 10 minutes

Cooking Time: 25 minutes

INGREDIENTS:

½ cup all-purpose flour, sifted
2½ teaspoons baking powder
½ teaspoon salt
1 tablespoon sugar
1½ cups corn meal
1 egg
3 tablespoons butter, melted
¾ cup milk

DIRECTIONS:

Preheat the oven to 425 degrees. Sift first four ingredients together. Stir in the corn meal.

In a separate bowl, beat the egg, then stir in the melted butter and milk. Combine with the flour mixture. Do not overmix; the batter will be lumpy.

Spoon into greased or papered muffin tins. Bake for 20 to 25 minutes.

✥

POACHED EGGS AND SAUSAGE WITH BILL'S SPECIAL SAUCE

Number of Servings: 6

Preparation Time: 10 minutes

Cooking Time: 15 minutes

INGREDIENTS:

    4 cups Bill's Special Sauce
    6 eggs
    6 patties sausage, cooked

DIRECTIONS:

Place the sauce in a 10 x 8 x 2-inch baking dish; cover with heavy-duty plastic wrap and microwave at high for 5 to 6 minutes, stirring after 3 minutes. Mixture should come to a boil.

Break eggs, one at a time, into a small bowl; gently slip each egg into the sauce. Pierce each yolk with a wooden pick. Cover with plastic wrap and microwave at medium-high for 6 to 7 minutes, or until egg whites are partially set. Let stand, covered, for 3 to 4 minutes. Meanwhile, place the sausage patties on a plate and cover with a paper towel. Then microwave on high for one minute or until hot.

Place the sausage patties on the serving plate. Carefully spoon eggs and sauce over the patties.

✜

RED BEANS

Number of Servings: 6

Preparation Time: 15 minutes, plus overnight soaking

Cooking Time: 45 minutes

INGREDIENTS:

    1 pound red beans
    10 cups cold water
    3-pound ham hock
    1 red chili pepper, chopped
    1 teaspoon salt
    1 large onion, chopped
    1 clove garlic, chopped
    4 tomatoes, chopped
    1 cup green bell peppers, chopped
    ½ teaspoon ground cumin
    1½ teaspoons chili pepper

DIRECTIONS:

Cover beans with cold water and soak overnight. Drain.

Place beans, ham hock, and the remaining ingredients in a 6-quart pressure cooker. Add enough water to cover the main ingredients. Close cover securely. Cook for 45 minutes.

Let the pressure cooker cool and remove the meat and bones from the beans. Break up any large chunks of meat and return the meat to beans. Dispose of the bone. Cool and refrigerate until ready to use. Tastes best the second heating.

✜

CHAPTER TWO

Luncheons

———————◆———————

A VICTORIAN TEA WITH RICHARD AND GLORIA MANNEY

Richard and Gloria Manney collected high-style Victorian furniture by John Henry Belter for twenty years, amassing one of the largest and most representative collections of works by this renowned American cabinetmaker. Recently, their Belter collections came to Winterthur on long-term loan, adding a new dimension to the museum's displays and leaving the Manneys with more room at home for their collections of Chippendale and Federal furniture, books, American landscape paintings, portrait miniatures, fans, and more.

Lavish is the best way to describe a Victorian tea with the Manneys. Opulently carved Belter furniture provides a suitable background for the sumptuous afternoon repast. The setting is made more memorable with elaborate repoussé silver, elegant floral-decorated porcelain, and finely cut glass. The floral centerpiece, of rose, spider plant, alstroemeria, and flowering dill, echoes the abundance for which the Victorian period was known.

Afternoon tea was more than a meal in Victorian times; it was a ritual and an important social occasion, when one served only the best to family and friends. This tradition is followed by the Manneys, who choose savories and sweets for their elegant

---

The silver repoussé teapot, ca. 1828, with its urn-shaped body, circular pedestal foot, and ivory handle, is from one of the earliest known beverage sets made by Samuel Kirk. A pressed glass bowl made in New England, ca. 1830, is perfect for jellies and jams. The hard-paste porcelain sauce boat, ca. 1740, painted with flowers and butterflies and steered by a seated figure, is one of a set from the Meissen Factory in Germany. The French porcelain teacups and saucers, ca. 1800, are part of a thirty-piece coffee service; they complement the Spode porcelain plates, ca. 1805, displayed in the Du Pont Dining Room at Winterthur.

meals. Tiny tea sandwiches of Smoked Salmon and dilled cream cheese, Miniature Puff Pastries filled with Almond Chicken Salad, Scones topped with sweet butter and jam, and Raspberry-Filled Shortbread highlight the fare.

On a cold afternoon, warm your guests with a sweet or smoky tea such as Earl Grey, Prince of Wales, or Darjeeling, or with a semi-dry sherry. In the summer, provide a cool diversion with lemony iced tea or a semi-sweet white wine, such as a German Kabinett.

Menu

Watercress Tea Sandwiches

Cucumber and Salmon Tea Sandwiches

Miniature Puff Pastries with Almond Chicken Salad

Scones with Jam and Sweet Butter

Raspberry Meringue Shortbread

Apricot Tartlets

Spiced Pecans

Dry Sherry

Tea

PREPARATION TIPS: SCONES

Much of this elegant afternoon tea can be prepared in advance, allowing you to adjust your teatime to meet the schedules of family and friends. Spiced pecans keep well for weeks if stored in a tight container and kept in a cool place. Shortbread, fruit tarts, and puff pastries can be made a day ahead and kept covered in a cool, dry place. Add the chicken salad to the puff pastries just before teatime!

Scones and tea sandwiches must be made and served fresh, as close to teatime as possible. To simplify this task, have all the sandwich fillings prepared and at room temperature before preparing the scone batter. Once you have a large batch of scones ready to go into the oven, set the batter aside for a minute and slice and butter the bread for the sandwiches. Assemble sandwich shapes while the scones are cooking.

When you remove the scones from the oven, transfer them to a napkin-lined basket or a serving dish. The scones should be allowed to cool for a few minutes before they are served, giving you time to put the finishing touches on the sandwich platter. But be sure to serve the scones warm, with lots of sweet butter, homemade fruit jams, and—if possible—clotted cream.

WATERCRESS TEA SANDWICHES

Yield: 24 small sandwiches

Preparation Time: 25 minutes

INGREDIENTS:

12 slices firm white bread
2 hard-boiled eggs
14–16 whole sprigs of watercress, washed and patted dry, saving a few for garnish
2 tablespoons mayonnaise
1 tablespoon prepared mustard

DIRECTIONS:

Cut bread into quarters and remove crusts. In medium bowl, mix coarsely chopped eggs and watercress that has been finely chopped. Add mayonnaise and mustard and blend well. Spread mixture on half of the bread quarters, topping each with a plain piece of bread and a sprig of watercress.

✣

CUCUMBER AND SALMON TEA SANDWICHES

Yield: 16 small sandwiches

Preparation Time: 25 minutes

INGREDIENTS:

8 slices light oat or wheat bread
2 tablespoons mayonnaise
2 ounces cream cheese
½ teaspoon fresh dill
Salt and pepper to taste
1 cucumber, thinly sliced
4 ounces salmon, thinly filleted

DIRECTIONS:

Cut bread into quarters and remove crusts. In small bowl mix mayonnaise and cream cheese, and season to taste with dill, salt, and pepper. Spread mixture on half of the bread quarters, topping each with a thin slice of cucumber, salmon, and a plain piece of bread.

MINIATURE PUFF PASTRIES WITH ALMOND CHICKEN SALAD

Yield: 24 pastries

Preparation Time: 35 minutes

Cooking Time: 20 to 25 minutes

INGREDIENTS:

Puff Pastry
1 cup water, very cold
½ cup butter, well chilled
1 teaspoon sugar
¼ teaspoon salt
1 cup sifted all-purpose flour
4 eggs

Almond Chicken Salad
1½ cups chicken, cooked and diced
½ cup almonds, slivered
⅓ cup mayonnaise
Lemon juice
Salt
Pepper

DIRECTIONS:

Puff Pastry—In a medium-size saucepan bring water, butter, sugar, and salt to full boil. Add flour all at once, stirring vigorously with a wire whisk. Mixture will form a thick, smooth ball that leaves sides of pan clean. Remove from heat and cool slightly. Add eggs one at a time, beating well after each addition. Paste will become shiny smooth. (As you add each egg, the paste will separate, but with continued beating it will smooth out.) Drop mixture by rounded teaspoonfuls onto a baking sheet. Bake in 400-degree oven for 20 to 25 minutes, or until puffed and golden brown. Cool on wire racks. When ready to fill, cut the tops off using a sharp paring knife.

Almond Chicken Salad—Combine chicken, almonds, mayonnaise, lemon juice, salt, and pepper. Place about a teaspoonful of the mixture into each prepared shell. Replace the tops. Garnish with fresh parsley and lemon slices.

Scones with Jam and Sweet Butter

Yield: 24 1-inch scones

Preparation Time: 25 to 30 minutes

Cooking Time: 10 to 15 minutes

INGREDIENTS:

1¼ cups flour
2½ teaspoons baking powder
¼ teaspoon salt
¼ cup butter
½ tablespoon honey
1 egg
¼ cup heavy cream
Granulated sugar

DIRECTIONS:

Preheat oven to 400 degrees. Sift together first three ingredients in large bowl. Cut in butter. In another bowl, mix honey, egg, and cream; add to dry mixture, but do not overwork. On lightly floured surface, roll dough into a circle ½ inch thick. Cut into rounds or triangles. Dip the tops of each scone into granulated sugar and bake on ungreased baking sheet for 10 to 15 minutes, until golden brown. Serve with jam and sweet butter.

✥

Raspberry Meringue Shortbread

Yield: 3 dozen cookies

Preparation Time: 25 minutes

Cooking Time: 35 minutes

INGREDIENTS:

1½ cups white flour
½ cup rice flour
½ cup sugar
2 egg yolks
¼ teaspoon salt
¾ cup butter

Topping
¼ teaspoon cinnamon
2 egg whites
½ cup sugar
½ cup raspberry jam
½ cup slivered blanched almonds

DIRECTIONS:

Preheat oven to 400 degrees. Sift white flour and rice flour together. Make a well in the center of the flour; add sugar, egg yolks, salt, and butter. Work together with hands until well blended. Press dough into ungreased square pan 9 x 9 x ¾ inches. Bake 15 or 20 minutes. Cool slightly and spread with raspberry jam.

Beat egg whites until foamy. Gradually add sugar and cinnamon. Continue beating until egg whites stand in stiff peaks. Spread meringue over jam; sprinkle with almonds. Bake 8 to 10 minutes, or until meringue is brown. Cut into 1½-inch squares.

✥

APRICOT TARTLETS

Yield: 24 2½-inch tarts

Preparation Time: 15 minutes, plus 45 minutes refrigeration

Cooking Time: 25 minutes

INGREDIENTS:

Tart Shells
1 cup butter, softened
1 cup sugar
2 egg yolks
1 teaspoon vanilla
2 tablespoons water
2 cups flour
1 teaspoon salt

Cheese Filling
1 8-ounce package cream cheese, softened
1 tablespoon confectioners' sugar
1 teaspoon milk
1 teaspoon lime rind

Fruit Glaze
1 16-ounce can halved apricots, drained, reserving
    ¾ cup juice and setting fruit aside
2 tablespoons sugar
1 tablespoon cornstarch

DIRECTIONS:

Tart Shells—Cream together butter and sugar until light and fluffy. In a separate bowl, beat together egg yolks, vanilla, and water. Combine egg mixture with creamed mixture, mixing thoroughly. Gradually sift in flour and salt. Knead until dough is smooth. Cover with a damp cloth and refrigerate for 45 minutes. When dough is ready, knead for a few minutes and roll out on a lightly floured board to a thickness of ⅛ inch. Cut dough into 3-inch circles and press into 2½-inch round tartlet tins. Prick the bottom and sides of the dough with a fork and bake in a 400-degree oven for 7 to 10 minutes or until golden brown. Cool thoroughly on wire racks before adding filling and glaze.

Cheese Filling—Beat all ingredients together. Spread a thin layer of the mixture into each tart shell. Place an apricot half in the center on top of the cheese filling.

Fruit Glaze—Mix together apricot juice, sugar, and cornstarch. Cook over medium heat, stirring constantly, until mixture thickens and becomes clear. Cool slightly and spoon over each fruit tart. Chill until ready to serve.

❖

SPICED PECANS

Yield: ½ pound

Preparation Time: 30 minutes

Cooking Time: 60 minutes

INGREDIENTS:

1 cup sugar
6 tablespoons cornstarch
1 tablespoon cinnamon
½ teaspoon ginger
½ teaspoon nutmeg
¼ teaspoon salt
½ pound pecans, shelled and halved
1 egg white

DIRECTIONS:

Combine sugar, cornstarch, and spices in small mixing bowl. Dip pecans into egg white and roll, one at a time, in spice mixture. Bake at 250 to 275 degrees for 1 hour. Cool completely. Store tightly covered or freeze.

MILDRED MOTTAHEDEH — A FABULOUS OFFICE LUNCHEON

For *businesswoman* Mildred Mottahedeh, president of Mottahedeh, Inc., a world-renowned manufacturer of porcelain and brass, working lunches are a necessity. Often on the go between her headquarters in New York and factories in Europe and China, Mrs. Mottahedeh has no time to waste and finds office meals with clients or staff both productive and refreshing.

For *collector* Mildred Mottahedeh, a beautiful place setting is a must. Over her many years of collecting, she has acquired one of the world's most acclaimed assemblages of Chinese export porcelain, and her passion for the porcelain continues to grow. Her collection features many pieces made in the eighteenth and early nineteenth centuries, when fledgling American factories were as yet unable to meet the growing demand for fine dinnerware.

This hearty office luncheon, featuring Lamb Stew with Garden Greens, Beet and Endive Salad, and Poached Pears, is interesting and unique, calling for a table setting that also exhibits these qualities.

Menu

Beet and Endive Salad with Mint Dressing

Lamb Stew with Garden Greens

Steamed Rice ‡

Pumpernickel Rolls ‡

Poached Pears

Coffee

Tea

‡ (recipe not included)

The Chinese export porcelain plates from Winterthur's fine collection, ca. 1800, depict the merchant ship Brilliante, *owned by a Portuguese trader based in Macao. Two-handled porcelain cups, ca. 1785, are hand-painted with the seal of the Society of the Cincinnati. The glassware, ca. 1820, also has the society's seal.*
Other items shown include Winterthur's Reed & Barton reproduction silverware, the original design ca. 1840, modern brass bread plates, and a modern cut-glass bowl.

PREPARATION TIPS: GREENS

Mention greens and most people think of salad. Traditionally, lettuce is the base for a garden salad, occasionally served with fresh herbs. In recent years, spinach salad has become popular and is now a staple at most salad bars. However, greens are really very versatile and need not be limited to use in salads, just as salads do not have to have lettuce or spinach as their base.

This menu stresses the innovative use of greens. A traditional lamb stew is given a tasty but unconventional twist with the addition of parsley, spinach, and iceberg lettuce, its flavor subtly enhanced with leeks, cinnamon, and nutmeg. In the accompanying salad, tart endive, rather than a blander lettuce, is the base for fresh julienned beets and a mint-and-mustard dressing.

Several varieties of greens are commonly available at markets and should be used freely. Bibb, Boston, green leaf, red leaf, Romaine, and oak leaf lettuce make an interesting change from iceberg; they can be used "wilted" or cooked in soups and stir-fried dishes as well as in salads. Chicory, arugula, escarole, and endive are also quite common at the market and are good as cooked greens. These are slightly bitter in taste and add interest in salads. Watercress and kale are becoming more popular as salad components.

A simple way to clean headed greens is to remove the core and run water into the opening. Leaves can also be removed and cleaned one by one. Loose greens, such as spinach, should be soaked, as they are often quite gritty and still have roots attached. If using the greens in a salad, be sure to dry them completely. Keep cleaned, thoroughly dried greens refrigerated until they are needed.

BEET AND ENDIVE SALAD WITH MINT DRESSING

Number of Servings: 8

Preparation Time: 25 minutes, plus 5 hours refrigeration

Cooking Time: 10 minutes

INGREDIENTS:

3 heads endive
4 fresh, medium-size beets, cooked, peeled, and julienned
8 sprigs fresh mint for garnish

Mint Dressing
½ cup lemon juice
½ cup vegetable oil
1 teaspoon Dijon mustard
8 mint leaves, chopped
Few sprigs dill

DIRECTIONS:

Separate the endive leaves by cutting off a small portion from the bottom of each head and loosening the leaves. Arrange leaves on individual plates, mounding beets in the center.

For dressing, combine ingredients together. Pour over beets and endive leaves. Garnish with mint sprigs.

LAMB STEW WITH GARDEN GREENS

Number of Servings: 8

Preparation Time: 20 minutes

Cooking Time: 1 hour

INGREDIENTS:

6½ tablespoons butter
2 medium onions, chopped
2 pounds lamb, cut into 1½-inch cubes
1½ teaspoons salt
½ teaspoon ground pepper
½ teaspoon cinnamon
½ teaspoon nutmeg
1¾ cups water
3 bunches green onions, chopped
3 leeks, chopped (firm white and light green parts)
1 bunch parsley, chopped
1 pound spinach, chopped
¼ head iceberg lettuce, chopped
1 can (16 ounces) kidney beans
3 tablespoons lemon juice
6 cups steamed rice

DIRECTIONS:

Melt 2½ tablespoons butter in a large, deep 4- to 6-quart pot. Add onions, lamb, and spices. Sauté mixture until meat is well browned. Add water and let simmer for 30 minutes. Sauté the green onions, leeks, parsley, spinach, and lettuce in 4 tablespoons butter for 5 minutes. Add vegetables and kidney beans to meat. Add lemon juice. Cook until meat is tender, about 20 minutes. Serve over steamed rice.

POACHED PEARS

Number of Servings: 8

Preparation Time: 10 minutes, plus 3–4 hours refrigeration

Cooking Time: 15 minutes

INGREDIENTS:

8 bosc pears
2 cups cranberry juice
2 cups apple juice
Mint leaves

DIRECTIONS:

Peel, core, and halve the pears. Mix the cranberry and apple juices. Heat the juices to the boiling point. Add pears and let simmer for about 15 minutes, or until pears begin to get soft. Chill for 3 to 4 hours. To serve, place pears in a pool of juice on individual plates. Garnish with fresh mint leaves.

LUNCH AT THE VICE PRESIDENT'S HOUSE WITH MRS. GEORGE BUSH

*V*ice President George Bush and Barbara Bush appreciate fine decorative arts. Antiques and special historical pieces that they collected have criss-crossed the country, as the Bushes have lived in nearly thirty houses in almost twenty cities in their forty years of marriage!

Their present home—the Vice President's House, a gracious Victorian home on the grounds of the Naval Observatory in Washington, D.C.—is filled with antique furniture and decorative arts, some donated by former Vice President Nelson Rockefeller, some on loan from the National Gallery of Art and other galleries, and some belonging personally to the Bushes. One of their favorite pieces is a Chinese chest purchased when they were posted in China.

Mrs. Bush entertains often at the Vice President's House. Despite her busy schedule, which includes attending many official functions and actively working on her special project to promote literacy in our country, she stays in touch with their five children and ten grandchildren. Mrs. Bush takes time to ensure a special visit to the Vice President's House for each guest. For a winter luncheon on such an occasion, Mrs. Bush might serve a piping hot seafood Casserole with Shrimp, Crab, Oysters, and Eggplant.

Menu

Beef Bouillon with Custard Rounds ‡

Tossed Green Salad ‡

Sliced Cold Beef Tenderloin

Shrimp, Crab, Oyster, and Eggplant Casserole

Cheese Platter

French Bread ‡

Old-Fashioned Vanilla Ice Cream

with Fresh Strawberries and Raspberries

Lace Cookies ‡

White Zinfandel

Coffee

‡ (recipes not included)

PREPARATION TIPS: SEAFOOD/EGGPLANT CASSEROLE

Seafood casserole makes an elegant appetizer for a special luncheon and is as delicious served at room temperature, on a bed of crisp Boston lettuce, as it is when served bubbling hot from the oven. It can also be used as a main course for supper, accompanied by a large tossed salad, crusty French bread, and crisply steamed vegetables.

By baking the eggplant first, cooking time for the seafood is reduced, decreasing the risk of its becoming tough and chewy. The eggplant and bread crumbs combine nicely to make a "crust" for the wonderful seafood layers, which are held together by a rich mixture of cheese and cream. This is most definitely not a dish for those watching their weight!

Mrs. Bush's recipe suggests baking the eggplant before peeling it, thereby killing two birds with one stone. However, when precooked eggplant is not needed, or if longer cooking time with other ingredients is desirable for flavor, there are quicker methods of peeling eggplant.

One method is to roast the eggplant over an open flame or burner, to loosen the skin. Cut a narrow slit in the peel, so that the eggplant will not pop when the skin is hot, and lance it with a long fork or shish kebab skewer. Hold the eggplant over the gas flame or lit burner until the skin becomes dark and discolored and begins to pull away from the body of the vegetable. Be sure to turn the eggplant frequently, as if roasting a marshmallow, so that it does not burn. Remove the vegetable from the heat, cool slightly, and peel.

Eggplant can also be braised whole in a heavy sauté or frying pan so that the skin will loosen for easy peeling. Be sure not to burn the pan. Turn the eggplant frequently until the skin has darkened almost to black. Let it cool before attempting to peel it.

Eggplant can taste bitter or hot if overcooked or if cooked with very hot seasonings. Take the afterbite of the eggplant into account and be sparing with red pepper and other seasonings.

The Society of the Cincinnati, founded by officers of the Revolutionary army in 1783, was an organization formed in the spirit of the young republic to perpetuate the friendship between American and French officers who fought together during the war. George Washington served as the society's first president. The insignia was designed by Major Pierre-Charles L'Enfant, who was later to lay out the new nation's capital.

Soon after the society's formation, porcelain bearing its insignia was ordered from China. George Washington purchased over three hundred pieces. Those the President did not buy form the bulk of Winterthur's Cincinnati collection, the largest single group of Cincinnati china in the country. Mottahedeh has reproduced the porcelain for today's use. Complementing the porcelain are glass goblets made in Wheeling, West Virginia, ca. 1820, also sporting the society's emblem.

The enamel boxes are of Winterthur designs made by Halcyon Days. The Winterthur reproduction shell-pattern flatware is manufactured by Reed & Barton.

SLICED COLD BEEF TENDERLOIN

Number of Servings: 8–10

Preparation Time: 10 minutes

Cooking Time: 1 hour

INGREDIENTS:

    1 beef tenderloin (4 pounds)
    Butter
    Pepper
    1 cup hot beef bouillon

DIRECTIONS:

Rub a trimmed fillet of beef with butter and pepper. Roast it in a 400-degree oven for 1 hour. Baste with bouillon for the first 30 minutes, then with the pan juices for the remaining roasting time. Allow the beef to cool thoroughly. Refrigerate overnight. Slice thinly and arrange attractively on a serving platter.

SHRIMP, CRAB, OYSTER, AND EGGPLANT CASSEROLE

Number of Servings: 8–10

Preparation Time: 25 minutes

Cooking Time: 1 hour, 20 minutes

INGREDIENTS:

    1 medium eggplant
    ½ cup butter
    ¾ cup chopped onions
    2 cloves garlic, pressed
    1 pound fresh mushrooms
    1 cup bread crumbs (French bread)
    ½ teaspoon black pepper
    Salt to taste
    1 teaspoon Old Bay Seasoning
    16 ounces backfin crab
    1 pound medium shrimp, boiled and shelled
    2 cups raw oysters
    ¾ cup light cream
    ½ cup sharp cheddar cheese, grated

DIRECTIONS:

Bake the eggplant in a 350-degree oven for 50 minutes, or until soft, by placing it in a baking dish with about a cup of water on the bottom. Slit the eggplant to keep from popping. Meanwhile sauté onions and garlic in butter until yellow, then add sliced mushrooms, ½ cup bread crumbs (reserve ½ cup), pepper, salt, and Old Bay Seasoning. Mix thoroughly and remove from heat. Peel and dice eggplant into 1-inch cubes.

Butter a 2- to 3-quart casserole dish and lay the eggplant on the bottom. Sprinkle with ¼ cup bread crumbs and one-half of the onion-mushroom mixture. Add a layer of crab, shrimp, and then oysters. Sprinkle with the remaining ¼ cup bread crumbs and remaining onion-mushroom mixture. Pour the light cream over the layers and top with grated cheese. Bake uncovered at 350 degrees for 15 minutes or until brown.

OLD-FASHIONED VANILLA ICE CREAM

Yield: 2½ quarts

Preparation Time: 10 minutes

Cooking Time: 10 minutes

INGREDIENTS:

6 egg yolks
1⅓ cups sugar
½ teaspoon salt
4 cups milk, scalded
2 cups heavy cream
3 tablespoons vanilla
Fresh strawberries
Fresh raspberries

DIRECTIONS:

Beat egg yolks with sugar and salt in a medium-size saucepan; stir in 2 cups of the milk. Heat slowly, stirring constantly, just until sugar dissolves. Remove from heat and add remaining milk and heavy cream. Blend. And cool. Pour mixture into the can of an ice cream maker. Prepare and freeze according to the manufacturer's directions.

Unsnap cranking gear; carefully wipe cover and around sides of can with a damp cloth. Lift off the lid and remove the dasher. Serve immediately with fresh strawberries and raspberries.

A MIDDAY LUNCHEON WITH AMBASSADOR AND MRS. WALTER ANNENBERG

Connoisseurs in every sense of the word, former Ambassador to the Court of St. James and Mrs. Walter Annenberg are consistently named among America's top collectors for their remarkable assemblage of French impressionist and post-impressionist art. To the Annenbergs, living with works of art is an important part of collecting them, and at Sunnylands, their estate in Palm Springs, California, they do just that.

Mr. and Mrs. Annenberg are also connoisseurs of entertaining, so much so that a visit to Sunnylands has become a New Year's tradition for President and Mrs. Reagan. An intimate lunch for four at Sunnylands is served with as much flair and attention to detail as a banquet for a head of state.

The Annenbergs' light but satisfying midday luncheon brings a cool respite from

the desert heat. Creamy chilled Artichoke Soup starts the meal, followed by classic Poached Salmon in aspic. Topping off the luncheon is a frozen vanilla Soufflé with a surprise—a core of creamy chocolate mousse.

Modern porcelain plates adapted from a Victorian dessert service and stately chairs from the Empire period contrast with the dramatic Oriental flower arrangement of spider mums, bamboo, and grasses. An exotic bamboo-print tablecloth has its counterpart in the prim white lace napkins.

Wine for this hot-weather dinner should be cool and light. Even a well-iced spritzer with a twist of lemon, or a tall, cool glass of minted iced tea would be most welcomed by guests.

Menu

Cold Artichoke Soup

Poached Salmon

Sweet and Sour Cucumbers

Russian Salad

Asparagus Vinaigrette

Soufflé Glacé Surprise

Pouilly-Fuissé

The plant-filled Conservatory at Winterthur is a perfect backdrop for Klismos-type mahogany-and-ash side chairs, ca. 1825. The chairs' gilt-stenciled crest-rail design is echoed by the rims of the porcelain fruit plates, reproduced by Mottahedeh. The melon-shaped covered dish and bread-stick containers are also part of this set.

Other items shown include an enamel lemon box, silverware in Reed & Barton's "Eighteenth Century" pattern, modern stemware, and a silver ice bucket courtesy of The Enchanted Owl.

Most people associate soup with winter, when hot pots on the stove steam kitchen windows and send warm, savory aromas throughout the house. But the pleasure of soup as a starter need not be restricted to cold weather. Well-chilled soups are the perfect beginning to any summer meal.

Many summer soups, such as gazpacho or borscht, are an appropriate main course for lunch or a light dinner. Cream-based soups, like those made with curried chicken or artichokes, are delicious served hot or cold. Fruit soups—cantaloupe, blueberry, cherry, and others—are just as wonderful for dessert as for a starter. Other easy and popular summer soups include jellied consommés, cold tomato soup with fresh herbs, and cucumber soup with yogurt and dill.

Many summer soups can be prepared without cooking, a boon to those stuck in the kitchen on a hot evening. Soft fruits and tender vegetables can be pureed and blended with cold stock, cream, or other bases, then seasoned with fresh herbs. Crisp or stringy vegetables and fruits should be cooked until soft and then pureed. Be sure to use the freshest ingredients available and use only fresh herbs whenever possible. Add herbs as a last step, just before pureeing and chilling the finished soup, so that the flavors are fresh and distinct.

Cold soups should be just that—very cold. Be sure to chill soup completely before serving. The soup will retain its temperature better if served in chilled bowls or, for informal occasions, in mugs. If it is to be served at the table, place the soup tureen in a larger dish lined with ice.

COLD ARTICHOKE SOUP

Number of Servings: 4–6

Preparation Time: 15 minutes, plus overnight refrigeration

Cooking Time: 30–40 minutes

INGREDIENTS:

2 tablespoons butter
½ small onion, chopped
8 fresh artichoke hearts
4 tablespoons flour
2 cups chicken stock
1 cup heavy cream
Salt and pepper to taste
Lemon slices and basil for garnish

DIRECTIONS:

In a medium-size saucepan melt butter and add onion. Cook onion until tender. Add artichokes, then flour, and mix well. Add chicken stock. Cook for 30 to 40 minutes, or until artichokes are soft. Blend well, strain, and add cream and seasoning. Refrigerate overnight.

If soup is too thick, add ½ cup milk while blending. A nice garnish would be a slice of lemon sprinkled with basil in each bowl. Pour the soup to serve.

❖

POACHED SALMON

Number of Servings: 4

Preparation Time: 35 minutes, plus overnight refrigeration

Cooking Time: 20 minutes

INGREDIENTS:

1 whole salmon (4–6 pounds)
4 ounces clam juice
4 cups water
¾ cup beef consommé

Aspic
1 envelope unflavored gelatin
1 8-ounce bottle clam juice
½ cup fish stock
Tomatoes, olives, leeks, truffles for garnish

DIRECTIONS:

Begin with a boned salmon wrapped in cheesecloth. Fill fish poacher with clam juice, water, and consommé. Add whole fish and bring to a boil, but do not boil. Reduce heat and poach for 20 minutes. Allow to cool for several hours or overnight in fish stock. Carefully transfer salmon onto a serving platter, skin side uppermost, and remove the skin. The skin on the head and tail should be left intact.

Aspic—Mix together unflavored gelatin, clam juice, and fish stock in a small saucepan. Heat on low until gelatin dissolves. Strain and refrigerate till cool but still liquid. Pour thin layer over the salmon, and let it set. Decorate the aspic with tomatoes, olives, leeks, or truffles. Pour more aspic over the decorations, and let dish set in the refrigerator until ready to serve.

Could be served with a mayonnaise-and-cognac sauce. Dark pumpernickel bread would be a nice accompaniment to the salmon.

❖

SWEET AND SOUR CUCUMBERS

Number of Servings: 4–6

*Preparation Time: 10 minutes, plus 30 minutes standing time,
2 hours refrigeration*

INGREDIENTS:

Salt
2 large cucumbers, peeled and thinly sliced
½ cup sugar
1 cup hot water
¼ cup white vinegar

Vinaigrette
½ tablespoon Dijon mustard
1 tablespoon lemon juice
1 tablespoon vinegar
¼ cup olive oil
¼ cup oil

DIRECTIONS:

Sprinkle cucumber slices with salt. Set aside for 30 minutes. Press the slices in your hand. In a small bowl mix sugar and hot water together. Add vinegar and cucumber slices. Let stand 2 hours in refrigerator and drain. Pat dry. Mix together vinaigrette ingredients with a whisk, and toss with cucumbers. Serve cold.

❖

RUSSIAN SALAD

Number of Servings: 4

Preparation Time: 25 minutes

Cooking Time: 7–10 minutes

INGREDIENTS:

¾ cup turnips, diced
¾ cup green beans, diced
¾ cup carrots, diced
¾ cup peas
¾ cup celery, diced
¾ cup mayonnaise
Freshly chopped parsley
Caviar for garnish

Optional: Beef tongue, diced ham, caviar, capers,
pickles, mushrooms, or lobster
Salt and pepper to taste

DIRECTIONS:

Cook all vegetables in large pot of boiling salted water for 7 to 10 minutes. Keep them crispy; do not overcook. Refresh cooked vegetables under cold running water for a few minutes. In large bowl, mix together vegetables, mayonnaise, and parsley. Add any of the optional ingredients and salt and pepper to taste. Decorate with sprinkles of caviar.

❖

ASPARAGUS VINAIGRETTE

Number of Servings: 4

Preparation Time: 10 minutes

Cooking Time: 7 minutes

INGREDIENTS:

1 to 1½ pounds fresh asparagus

Vinaigrette
1 tablespoon Dijon mustard
2 tablespoons lemon juice
2 tablespoons vinegar
½ cup olive oil
½ cup vegetable oil
Salt and pepper to taste
Lemon zest to garnish

DIRECTIONS:

Peel and clean asparagus. Cook in salted boiling water for about 7 minutes, keeping asparagus firm. Refresh under cold water. Drain on paper towels. Whisk together all ingredients for vinaigrette; add salt and pepper to taste.

Place asparagus on plate and pour on vinaigrette; garnish with lemon zest.

❖

SOUFFLÉ GLACÉ SURPRISE

Number of Servings: 6–8

Preparation Time: 40 minutes

Cooking Time: 20 minutes, plus 8 hours freezing time

INGREDIENTS:

Vanilla Soufflé
2 cups milk
16 egg yolks
2 cups sugar
1 teaspoon vanilla
2 cups heavy cream, whipped

Chocolate Mousse
1 8-ounce bar semisweet chocolate, melted
2 egg whites, beaten
1 cup heavy cream, firmly beaten

DIRECTIONS:

Vanilla Soufflé—In a medium saucepan, bring milk to a boil, then remove from heat. In a separate bowl, mix eggs and sugar until well blended. Add vanilla and 1 cup of the heated milk. Blend. Return mixture to saucepan with remaining cup of milk, and cook on a very low heat until mixture coats the back of a wooden spoon. Do not overcook. Strain and set aside in refrigerator to cool, about 15 to 20 minutes. When cold add whipped cream and mix well. Prepare a 2-quart soufflé dish with a collar of wax paper. Pour into dish. Freeze for 5 to 6 hours.

Chocolate Mousse—Mix together melted chocolate and beaten egg whites. Fold in whipped cream. With a spoon, remove enough from the center of the vanilla soufflé to accommodate the chocolate mousse mixture. Fill the center with the chocolate mixture. Re-cover the top with soufflé mixture and return to freezer for 2 more hours. Do not overfreeze.

CHAPTER THREE

Cocktails and Hors d'Oeuvres

---◆---

DESSERT BUFFET AFTER THE AUCTION WITH WENDELL AND BETSY GARRETT

Antiques and art play an important and very special role in the lives of Mr. and Mrs. Wendell D. Garrett. Wendell Garrett is the editor of *The Magazine Antiques*, internationally recognized as a leading publication in the field. Betsy Garrett is associate director of the American Arts Course at Sotheby's, a part of that company's acclaimed "Works of Art" connoisseurship training program. Both appreciate meeting with friends after an auction—to unwind, to celebrate the setting of new price records, or to discuss trends in collecting and upcoming sales.

This Garrett post-auction gathering allows a sampling of the sinfully delicious desserts that make up the buffet fare. One of Mrs. Garrett's favorites is buttery, melt-in-the-mouth Shortbread Cookies, teamed here with delicate Chocolate Lace Cookies and sweet-and-sour Lemon Squares. Rich Amaretto Cheesecake, Almond Torte, and a decadent filled Chocolate Roll comprise the rest of the buffet.

Two tables are laid out, allowing guests easy access to flavorful coffee and luscious desserts. A side table holds dishes and cutlery, as well as coffee and a selection of cookies. Additional desserts are placed on a larger table. Both are highlighted by exquisite nineteenth-century French porcelain, gilded and embellished with a colorful tassel and vine pattern. A graceful silver service holds coffee, rich cream, and sugar. Flowers on the side table are simple, but stately. Reflected in the looking glass, they add additional depth and color to the room.

Reflected in the gilded mirror, ca. 1830, made by Benjamin Spencer of Philadelphia, are tulips and cherry blossoms from the Winterthur gardens. The flowers are displayed in a French porcelain gilded vase, ca. 1815. A luscious buffet is set up on the marble-topped pier table, made by Michael Allison of New York ca. 1816. The silver teapot, sugar dome, and creamer, ca. 1800, were all made by Joseph Richardson, Jr., of Philadelphia. The porcelain dessert service was brought to New York about 1836 by Eugene Lentilhon, the great-great-uncle of Henry Francis du Pont.

59

Good food and conversation are the perfect transition between an exciting evening of sales and the quiet hours of nighttime. Accompany this lavish fare with an assortment of liqueurs or a mellow port wine. Hot, specially blended coffee is also a must with this "meal."

Menu

Amaretto Cheesecake

Chocolate Roll

Almond Torte

Cookie Plate:

Shortbread Cookies

Lemon Squares

Chocolate Lace Cookies

Demitasse

Tea

PREPARATION TIP: COFFEE

Even the most spectacular dessert buffet is not complete without freshly brewed coffee. Several excellent varieties are widely available, as are top-quality home coffee grinders and coffee-making systems.

Choose coffees to accompany particular foods according to personal preference. The body, richness, and aftertaste of the brew will vary according to the type and roast of the bean. Roast generally falls into one of four categories, popularly known as American, Vienna, French, and espresso or Italian.

American roast, used widely by American coffee manufacturers, is fairly light and mild. Medium-dark coffee, richer than American but still smooth and mild, is often called Vienna roast. French roast is dark chocolate brown in color and produces a very deep, full-bodied brew. The darkest roast, espresso, is almost black and produces a very strong brew with a slightly acidic aftertaste.

Coffees called "Arabica," "Mocha-Java," "Malabar," "Kenya," "Hawaiian Kona," or by some other geographic name are designated not by the roast but according to the origin of the beans. Among the most sought-after and expensive are the Jamaican Blue Mountain and High Mountain beans, grown in very small quantities in the mountains of Jamaica. The mellow, full-bodied coffee they produce is cherished by experts and gourmets throughout the world. These beans can be found, in small and costly bags, at many gourmet stores.

More widely available, and exceptionally good, are coffees from Colombia, Brazil, Costa Rica, and Kenya. All are made from high-quality beans that produce consistently rich and good brews. Mocha-Java, a blend of North African mocha beans and Indonesian java beans, is medium- to rich-bodied, depending on the proportion of beans used (the mocha beans are heavier than the java). Hawaiian Kona and lesser-known Puerto Rican beans produce a light, mild brew with a smooth aftertaste.

Almost everyone has a preferred method of brewing coffee. All methods of brewing will benefit from these tips:

- Store coffee unground in the freezer and grind enough for each pot just before brewing. If you use a blade grinder, set it for a pulse action similar to a food processor's. This saves both the blade and the beans.
- Brew regular-strength coffee with 2 tablespoons of coffee for each 6-ounce cup. Strong coffee takes 3 tablespoons of grounds for each 6-ounce cup.
- Serve coffee with cream that is at room temperature or just below it, so that it does not overcool the drink. Be sure the cream is fresh; old cream may curdle when it is served warm.
- Serve espresso with a twist of lemon and sugar, if desired—but never with cream!

AMARETTO CHEESECAKE

Yield: 9-inch cake

Preparation Time: 30 minutes

Cooking Time: 1 hour, 20 minutes

INGREDIENTS:

Crust
1 cup flour
¼ cup sugar
1 teaspoon lemon rind, grated
1 egg yolk
½ cup butter

Filling
2½ pounds cream cheese
1¾ cups sugar
3 tablespoons flour
1½ teaspoons lemon rind
1 tablespoon lemon juice
½ teaspoon vanilla
¼ cup amaretto
5 eggs
2 egg yolks
¼ cup heavy cream
¼ cup slivered almonds, toasted

DIRECTIONS:

Crust—Combine flour, sugar, and lemon rind in a large mixing bowl. Make a well in the center and add the yolk and butter. Work mixture until well blended, adding a little cold water, if necessary, to make a light dough. Wrap the dough in wax paper and chill for at least 1 hour. Roll the dough out to a ⅛-inch thickness. Oil the bottom only of a 9-inch springform pan and trim the dough to fit the circle. Bake the circle in a 400-degree oven until it is lightly browned, about 5 to 6 minutes. Butter the sides of the pan and clamp onto base, including cooked dough. Roll out the remaining dough to a thickness of ⅛ inch and make a band to fit around sides of the pan, pressing firmly against the bottom crust. Add filling.

Filling—Combine cream cheese, sugar, flour, lemon rind, lemon juice, vanilla, and amaretto in a large mixing bowl. Blend well and add whole eggs and the yolks, one at a time, beating lightly after each addition. Fold in heavy cream. Pour filling into crust. Bake the cheesecake for 12 minutes at 400 degrees. Reduce temperature to 300 degrees and bake for 1 hour. Sprinkle with toasted almonds. Allow the cheesecake to cool before slicing it.

❖

CHOCOLATE ROLL

Number of Servings: 6–8

Preparation Time: 20 minutes, plus 1 hour refrigeration time

Cooking Time: 15 minutes

INGREDIENTS:

2 teaspoons butter
6 ounces sweet chocolate
2 tablespoons water
1 tablespoon oil
1 teaspoon vanilla

5 egg yolks
⅔ cup sugar
5 egg whites, stiffly beaten
½ cup confectioners' sugar
1 cup heavy cream, whipped

DIRECTIONS:

Butter an 11″ x 17″ jelly-roll pan and line it with wax paper. Butter the wax paper.

Together in a small saucepan, over medium-high heat, melt chocolate in the water and oil. Remove from heat, add vanilla, and mix until smooth. Set aside. Preheat oven to 350 degrees.

Beat the egg yolks and add sugar, beating until thick and light. Stir in chocolate mixture. Fold in the egg whites. Spread mixture evenly in the prepared pan and bake for 15 minutes. (Do not overbake; cake should be fairly moist.) Cover with a damp cloth and refrigerate for 1 hour. Sprinkle confectioners' sugar on a piece of wax paper and turn cake out on it. Spread cake with whipped cream. Roll cake up like a jelly roll. Chill before serving.

✥

ALMOND TORTE

Number of Servings: 6
Preparation Time: 25 minutes
Cooking Time: 10–14 minutes

INGREDIENTS:

Cake
1 cup ground almonds
1 cup sugar
¾ cup butter
½ cup flour

Filling
1 cup milk or light cream
2 tablespoons sugar
2 teaspoons cocoa
2 heaping teaspoons cornstarch
1 cup whipped cream
¼ cup semisweet chocolate, grated

DIRECTIONS:

Cake—Mix all ingredients together and divide into 4 portions. Bake each portion in a no. 6 iron frying pan, pressing down to cover bottom of pan. Bake in a 350-degree oven until light brown. Be sure to let each cake get cold before removing from the pan.

Filling—Mix first four ingredients together in a saucepan. Bring to a boil over medium-high heat. Cook until thick. Cool. Fold in ½ cup whipped cream. Spread this mixture between each of the cake layers. Cover the top with ½ cup whipped cream and sprinkle with grated chocolate.

✥

SHORTBREAD COOKIES

Yield: 24 cookies

Preparation Time: 15 minutes

Cooking Time: 25–30 minutes

INGREDIENTS:

- 2 sticks unsalted (sweet) butter
- ¾ cup dark brown sugar, firmly packed
- ¾ teaspoon salt
- 2 cups all-purpose flour, unbleached

DIRECTIONS:

Soften butter. Cream the butter and add the sugar and salt, beating the mixture with an electric mixer until it is fluffy. Add the flour, ⅓ cup at a time, mixing by hand. Divide the dough into 4 parts and arrange 2 of these parts on each of 2 buttered baking sheets. Flatten the 4 parts into 4-inch rounds and mark each into 6 wedges by pricking with the tines of a fork. Bake the rounds in a preheated oven at 300 degrees for 25 to 30 minutes, or until they are just firm to the touch. While rounds are still warm, trace along the fork marks with a knife without cutting all the way through. Let the cookies cool on the baking sheets and break them into wedges.

✚

LEMON SQUARES

Yield: 30 squares

Preparation Time: 20 minutes

Cooking Time: 30 minutes

INGREDIENTS:

- ¾ cup butter
- ½ cup confectioners' sugar, sifted
- 1½ cups all-purpose flour
- ½ cup cornstarch
- 1 cup sweetened condensed milk
- ½ cup lemon juice
- 2 egg yolks
- 2 egg whites
- ¼ cup sugar
- ⅓ cup coconut, shredded
- ⅛ cup confectioners' sugar for sprinkling on top

DIRECTIONS:

In a mixing bowl, cream together the butter and confectioners' sugar. Gradually work in the flour and cornstarch. Press into a greased 9″ x 11″ oblong cake pan and bake in a 350-degree oven for 15 minutes. Mix the condensed milk, lemon juice, and egg yolks. Spread mixture on top of the cooked first layer. Whip the egg whites until they are stiff. Gradually beat in the sugar and fold in the coconut. Spread over the filling and bake for another 15 minutes. Cut into squares when fully cooled. Sprinkle with confectioners' sugar.

✚

CHOCOLATE LACE COOKIES

Yield: 48 cookies

Preparation Time: 20 minutes

Cooking Time: 5–6 minutes

INGREDIENTS:

Cookies
1 cup flour, sifted
1 cup walnuts, finely chopped
½ cup corn syrup
½ cup shortening
⅔ cup brown sugar, packed

Chocolate Icing
1 4-ounce package German sweet chocolate
3 tablespoons butter
1½ cups confectioners' sugar, sifted
3 tablespoons hot water

DIRECTIONS:

Cookies—In a small mixing bowl, blend flour and chopped walnuts. Preheat oven to 375 degrees. In a saucepan, over medium heat, bring corn syrup, shortening, and sugar to a boil, stirring constantly. Remove from heat; gradually stir in flour mixture. Drop batter by level teaspoonfuls about 3 inches apart on a lightly greased baking sheet. Bake for 5 to 6 minutes; remove from oven and allow to stand 5 minutes before removing from baking sheet.

Icing—In a saucepan, over low heat, melt chocolate and butter. Remove from heat; stir in confectioners' sugar and hot water. Add more hot water if too stiff. Drizzle each cookie with the icing.

A SPRING WINE-TASTING PARTY AT THE CHADDSFORD WINERY

The Chaddsford Winery, a mere five miles from the Winterthur estate, produces some of the finest wines of the Brandywine Valley—indeed, of the entire mid-Atlantic region. Proprietor-vintner Eric Miller's passion for wine and his quest for knowledge about the "nectar of the gods" show in the exceptional vintages he produces.

Seeking the most appropriate setting for his offspring has led Mr. Miller to develop two other areas of expertise. First, he collects "country" antique furnishings—the rustic tables, chairs, rugs, and accessories that have the same rural origins as his wines. Second, he has developed a knowledge of the foods that will complement his wines, especially the local foods that best reflect the region from which the wine comes.

This spring wine-tasting party menu is designed to satisfy the most discriminating palate. The foods that have been chosen uniquely complement the wines, and many

of them are local in origin. Mushrooms from nearby Kennett Square, Pennsylvania, the "mushroom capital of the world," are served as an appetizer with a light, white spring wine whose slightly sweet, slightly crisp taste is balanced by the mild, savory legume. Another appetizer suggested is mild local goat cheese served on Garlic Toast Rounds. A dry, delicate Seyval Blanc accompanies Chesapeake Crab Salad, mildly seasoned for a piquant flavor.

Grilled Spring Chicken, seasoned only with pepper, soy sauce, and sage, is served with Chardonnay, dry and delicate but with a subtle undertone of honey and nuts. A full-bodied wine, Chardonnay can accompany even rich foods. A spicier Chambourcin, reminiscent of the hearty red wines of northern Italy and the Rhone Valley, is served with the Roast Veal Nouveau.

Dessert is limited to Melon Balls in Port, garnished with mint leaves. If desired, butter cookies or tea biscuits may be served with this course. No accompanying wine is needed with this light but satisfying finale.

Be sure to serve a lemon sorbet between the appetizers and the main course. It will cleanse the palate so that guests can savor fully the varied wines to follow.

PREPARATION TIP: SEASONINGS

The key to cooking foods to accompany fine wines is to use a light but creative hand with seasonings. Wine is enhanced by appropriate seasonings, but overwhelmed by too much or the wrong flavor.

This menu suggests mild seasonings throughout, even for foods usually served quite spicy. Chesapeake crab salad should have only a hint of Old Bay Seasoning. Eric Miller suggests cutting the usual amount of seasoning by three-quarters. Roast veal nouveau is lightly flavored with garlic, oregano, honey, and nouveau wine, forgoing heavier spices. Melon balls with port relies only on the fruit, wine, and delicate fresh mint for its flavor.

The key to seasoning here is *fresh*. Use only fresh, good-quality ingredients. If purchased dried, herbs and spices should be stored in a cool, dark place and should be replaced periodically, even if they are not used up. Buy Parmesan cheese in a block and grate it fresh, storing any unused cheese, tightly covered, in the refrigerator. Buy garlic in heads and press the cloves individually, with either a garlic press or a wide-bladed knife. Do not rely on garlic powder.

For cheeses and garlic, recipes will use less of the fresh product than of the packaged or processed. For herbs, use up to twice as much fresh as dry for equally strong seasoning.

The reflecting pool behind Winterthur is the perfect setting for this wine-tasting party.
A bellflower-and-leaf-border Wedgwood earthenware, ca. 1771, from England, is the focal point for this enjoyable event. The reproduction flatware pattern, "Winterthur," adapted from a dinner fork in the museum's Ineson-Bissell Silver Collection, has a scallop-shell design repeated on the reverse of every handle. Modern tall flutes, plus bell-shaped stemware and intricate silver candelabra, are perfect to show off the wonderful Chaddsford wines.

Menu

Feta Cheese on Garlic Toast Rounds

Mushroom Caps with Parmesan Cheese

Chesapeake Crab Salad

Boneless Grilled Chicken

Roast Veal Nouveau

Stuffed Onions

Melon Balls with Port

Seyval Blanc

Chardonnay

Chambourcin

FETA CHEESE ON GARLIC TOAST ROUNDS

Yield: 1 loaf

Preparation Time: 15 minutes

Cooking Time: 15 minutes

INGREDIENTS:

1 loaf French bread, thinly sliced
Garlic powder
Butter
1 package feta cheese

DIRECTIONS:

Toast bread, which has been spread with butter and sprinkled with garlic. Spread toasted bread with plenty of feta cheese and serve immediately.

MUSHROOM CAPS WITH PARMESAN CHEESE

Yield: 25–30 mushrooms

Preparation Time: 10 minutes

Cooking Time: 5–6 minutes

INGREDIENTS:

1½ pounds fresh mushrooms
4 tablespoons butter
¾ to 1 cup fresh Parmesan cheese, coarsely grated
Parsley
Green straw

DIRECTIONS:

Clean mushrooms and remove stems. Place caps on a broiler-proof pan and fill the wells with pats of butter. Broil until tender, about 5–6 minutes. Remove from oven and fill caps with Parmesan cheese. Serve hot or at room temperature. Garnish serving plate with parsley and green straw.

CHESAPEAKE CRAB SALAD

Number of Servings: 12

Preparation Time: 25 minutes

INGREDIENTS:

Pinch of salt
2 tablespoons vinegar
10 tablespoons oil
Pepper to taste
2 medium onions, chopped
2 pounds lump crabmeat
4 medium tomatoes, cubed
4 tablespoons capers
1½ cups mayonnaise
2 heads lettuce, romaine or Bibb

DIRECTIONS:

Dissolve a pinch of salt in the vinegar. Add the oil and pepper to taste. Stir in the chopped onions. Set aside. Place the crabmeat in a large mixing bowl. Add the tomatoes and capers. Mix eight tablespoons of the mayonnaise with the oil and vinegar mixture. Toss lightly into the crab and tomato mixture. Line 12 individual salad plates or bowls with lettuce leaves and fill with the crab salad. Place a spoonful of the remaining mayonnaise on top of each salad.

BONELESS GRILLED CHICKEN

Number of Servings: 12

Preparation Time: 10 minutes

Cooking Time: 15–25 minutes

INGREDIENTS:

Grapevine cuttings for grilling
½ cup oil
¼ cup soy sauce
Fresh ground black pepper
½ cup sage leaves, fresh and lightly packed
12 boneless chicken breasts
Grape leaves and sage sprigs for garnish

DIRECTIONS:

Prepare outdoor grill by laying grapevine cuttings on top of hot coals. In a mixing bowl, combine oil, soy sauce, pepper, and sage leaves (pressing leaves against side of bowl). Dip chicken into sage sauce, reserving the rest to use for basting while the chicken cooks. Grill chicken breasts for 15 to 25 minutes or until they are no longer pink on the inside. Serve on a bed of grape leaves and fresh sage sprigs.

ROAST VEAL NOUVEAU

Number of Servings: 12

Preparation Time: 15–20 minutes

Cooking Time: 3 hours, 15 minutes

INGREDIENTS:

8-pound boneless veal rump or sirloin roast
4 teaspoons salt
1 teaspoon pepper
16 cloves garlic, crushed
6 teaspoons oil
1 cup nouveau wine
½ cup chicken stock
4 teaspoons oregano, crumbled
1 teaspoon honey

DIRECTIONS:

Rub surface of roast with salt and pepper. Place roast on rack in an open shallow roasting pan. Do not add water or cover. Roast in 350-degree oven for two hours. In a small saucepan, gently simmer remaining ingredients (except for the wine) for 15 minutes. Remove from heat and add the wine. Pour the sauce mixture over the roast and continue cooking, covered, for about one hour. Occasionally baste the roast with the sauce. For a well-done roast, the meat thermometer should register 170 degrees.

STUFFED ONIONS

Number of Servings: 12

Preparation Time: 25 minutes

Cooking Time: 25–30 minutes

INGREDIENTS:

12 small Spanish onions
Salt and pepper
8 tablespoons butter
8 tablespoons flour
5 cups spinach, cooked and strained
1 cup sour cream
8 mushrooms, finely chopped
2 cups heavy cream
4 tablespoons butter
2 egg yolks
2 teaspoons flour
2 tablespoons brandy
½ cup Swiss cheese, grated
½ cup Parmesan cheese, grated
Bread crumbs
Parsley, chopped

DIRECTIONS:

Skin the onions and parboil them in a medium-size saucepan. Pull the centers of each onion out, leaving the two outer layers intact. Season with salt and pepper, inside and out. Place ½ teaspoon of butter inside each onion and place in a shallow baking dish. Melt the remainder of the 8 tablespoons of butter in a pan and stir in the flour. Cook slowly and add the strained spinach. Add the sour cream, salt, and pepper, and cook for about five minutes. Fill each onion with the spinach mixture. In a small saucepan, mix together the finely chopped mushrooms, heavy cream, 4 tablespoons of butter, salt, and pepper. Bring quickly to a boil. In another bowl, mix the egg yolks with the 2 tablespoons of flour and brandy. Add this to the cream mixture. Stir until the sauce thickens, but do not let it boil. Pour ½ of this mixture over the onions, sprinkle the tops with the grated Swiss cheese, then pour over the rest of the sauce. Sprinkle with Parmesan cheese and bread crumbs; dot with butter. Brown under the broiler and garnish with chopped parsley. Serve at once.

❖

MELON BALLS WITH PORT

Number of Servings: 12

Preparation Time: 30 minutes

INGREDIENTS:

4 ripe honeydew melons, halved and seeded
4 ripe cantaloupe melons, halved and seeded
12 ounces port wine
12 mint leaves for garnish

DIRECTIONS:

With a melon baller, scoop out balls from the melons and place them in a large bowl. Have ready 12 stemmed dessert glasses. Refrigerate melon balls until ready to serve. Just before serving, portion the melon balls out equally and pour about 1 ounce of port on top of each serving. Garnish with a sprig of mint.

CHAPTER FOUR

Dinners

—————◆—————

CRAIG CLAIBORNE'S MISSISSIPPI YANKEE DINNER

*I*n the tried-and-true American way, Craig Claiborne's Mississippi Yankee dinner combines northern and southern traditions in a most ingenious and charming manner. Originally conceived for a dinner in honor of Winterthur held at Christie's in New York City, the menu includes some of America's best contributions to culinary tradition: Oyster Stew, Shrimp Creole with Creole Rice, and Southern Pecan Pie, to name but a few.

The table setting in Winterthur's Queen Anne Dining Room reflects the subtle combination of color, texture, form, and scent essential to any memorable meal. Rare aubergine porcelain made in England in the eighteenth century highlights the table, which also features the finest American silver, glass, linens, and—of course—flowers.

Only a connoisseur could create a menu worthy of such a setting, and Mr. Claiborne is a connoisseur indeed. Long recognized as a culinary taste-setter, Mr. Claiborne has helped bring American cuisine to its present immense popularity around the world through his renowned cookbooks and his acclaimed writings in the *New York Times*. One of Winterthur's most ardent supporters, Mr. Claiborne has written a feature article about the museum for *National Geographic Traveler*. His appreciation

—————

The Queen Anne Dining Room at Winterthur forms a perfect background for the walnut New York dinner table, ca. 1730. The Queen Anne chairs, ca. 1730, also from New York, are covered in blue resist-dyed white linen from England and add color to an extravagant array of rare aubergine earthenware.

Antiques shown include eighteenth-century tin-glazed earthenware from England; an earthenware mustard pot, ca. 1700; a porcelain reclining figurine, ca. 1700; silver candlesticks, ca. 1720, made by Nathaniel Morse of Boston; English silver knives, ca. 1780; English silver plate forks, ca. 1773; and silver spoons, ca. 1760, made by Louis Feuter of New York.

of Winterthur stems from his love of America's culinary and cultural heritage.

This dinner was first served with a choice of wines suggested by Mr. Claiborne. You too can choose from his recommendations—a Chardonnay or a Cabernet Sauvignon, both from California—or select an alternative.

Menu

American Caviar with Toast Points ‡

Oyster Stew

Paul Prudhomme's Shrimp Creole

Creole Rice

Field Salad

American Goat Cheese

Southern Pecan Pie with Whipped Cream

Stratford 1984 Chardonnay

Roudon Smith Vineyards 1981

Cabernet Sauvignon

---

‡ (recipe not included)

PREPARATION TIPS: SHELLFISH

Overcooked shellfish is tough, chewy, and thoroughly unpleasant, making seafood dishes like shrimp creole and oyster stew difficult to prepare in advance. To overcome this problem, you can prepare these dishes in stages—the base or broth ahead of time, with the finishing touches added just before serving. Add shrimp or oysters at the very last minute and cook them only long enough to heat them through.

If you are serving seafood cold, be sure to serve it thoroughly chilled. If necessary, place the serving dish in a larger ice-lined dish to maintain the chill. For chilled shrimp, crab, and lobster, or for raw clams, oysters, and mussels, try sauces that go beyond the traditional spiced cocktail and tartar sauces. Mayonnaise-thickened hollandaise sauce, dill-yogurt dips, lemon sauces, and other herb/mayonnaise and tomato-based sauces provide an interesting change. Any flavor, like garlic, wine, or oregano, used in seasoning a hot shellfish dish will be good incorporated into a sauce for chilled shellfish.

OYSTER STEW

Number of Servings: 8

Preparation Time: 10–15 minutes

Cooking Time: 10–15 minutes

INGREDIENTS:

6 cups milk
6 bay leaves
6 stalks of celery with leaves
6 small onions, peeled and quartered
4 sprigs fresh thyme, or 1 teaspoon dried
24–48 oysters, 2–3 cups, depending on oyster size and
    portion to be served
Salt to taste
1½ cups heavy cream
2 egg yolks
Tabasco sauce to taste
1 teaspoon celery salt
Freshly ground pepper to taste
4 tablespoons butter
1 teaspoon Worcestershire sauce, optional
Oyster crackers

DIRECTIONS:

Combine the milk, bay leaves, celery, onions, and thyme in a saucepan. Bring just to the boil, but do not boil. Pour the oysters into a deep skillet large enough to hold the stew. Sprinkle with salt and bring to the boil. Cook just until the oysters curl. Strain the milk over the oysters and stir. Discard the solids. Do not boil.

Beat the cream with the egg yolks and add the Tabasco, celery salt, and salt and pepper to taste. Add to the stew. Bring just to the boil and swirl in the butter. Add the Worcestershire and serve piping hot with buttered toast or oyster crackers.

✣

PAUL PRUDHOMME'S SHRIMP CREOLE

Number of Servings: 8

Preparation Time: 30–35 minutes

Cooking Time: 1 hour to 1 hour, 10 minutes

INGREDIENTS:

3 pounds large shrimp with heads and shells, as fatty as possible
2½ cups basic shrimp stock
¼ cup chicken fat, pork lard, or beef fat
2½ cups onions, finely chopped
1¾ cups celery, finely chopped
1½ cups green bell peppers, finely chopped
4 tablespoons unsalted butter
2 teaspoons garlic, minced
1 bay leaf
2 teaspoons salt
1½ teaspoons white pepper
1 teaspoon ground red pepper (preferably cayenne)
¾ teaspoon black pepper
1½ teaspoons Tabasco sauce
1 tablespoon dried sweet basil leaves
3 cups tomatoes, peeled and finely chopped (preferably Creole)
1½ cups canned tomato sauce
2 teaspoons sugar
6 cups hot basic cooked rice

DIRECTIONS:

Rinse and peel shrimp; refrigerate until needed. Use heads and shells to make basic shrimp stock. Heat the chicken or other fat over high heat in a 4-quart saucepan until melted. Add 1 cup of the onions and cook over high heat for 3 minutes, stirring frequently. Lower the heat to medium-low and continue cooking, stirring frequently, until onions are a rich brown color but not burned, about 3 to 5 minutes. Add the remaining 1½ cups onions, the celery, bell peppers, and butter. Cook over high heat until the bell peppers and celery start to get tender, about 5 minutes, stirring occasionally.

Add garlic, bay leaf, salt, and peppers; stir well. Then add the Tabasco, basil, and ½ cup of the stock. Cook over medium heat for about 5 minutes to allow seasonings to marry and vegetables to brown further, stirring occasionally and scraping pan bottom well. Add the tomatoes; turn heat to low and simmer 10 minutes, stirring occasionally and scraping pan bottom. Stir in the tomato sauce and simmer 5 minutes, stirring occasionally. Add the remaining 2 cups of stock and the sugar. Continue simmering sauce for 15 minutes, stirring occasionally.

Cool and refrigerate sauce if it is made the day before. If serving immediately, turn heat off and add the shrimp; cover the pot and let sit just until shrimp are plump and pink, about 5 to 10 minutes. Meanwhile, heat the serving plates in a 250-degree oven. To serve, center ½ cup mounded rice on each heated serving plate; spoon 1 cup of the shrimp creole sauce around the rice and arrange 8 or 9 shrimp on the sauce.

CREOLE RICE

Number of Servings: 6 cups

Preparation Time: 15 minutes

Cooking Time: 1 hour, 10 minutes

INGREDIENTS:

2 cups uncooked rice (preferably converted)
2½ cups seafood stock
1½ tablespoons onion, very finely chopped
1½ tablespoons celery, very finely chopped
1½ tablespoons green bell pepper, very finely chopped
1½ tablespoons unsalted butter, melted
½ teaspoon salt
⅛ teaspoon garlic powder
Pinch each of white, cayenne, and black pepper

DIRECTIONS:

In a 5″ x 9″ x 2½″ pan, combine all ingredients; mix well. Seal pan snugly with aluminum foil. Bake at 350 degrees until rice is tender, about 1 hour, 10 minutes. Serve immediately.

If rice is to be made ahead of time and stored, omit the bell peppers—they tend to sour quickly.

© 1984 Paul Prudhomme. From *Chef Paul Prudhomme's Louisiana Kitchen* (New York: William Morse & Co., 1984), p. 224.

❖

FIELD SALAD

Number of Servings: 8

Preparation Time: 10 minutes

INGREDIENTS:

1½ cups dandelion greens
1½ cups spinach leaves
1½ cups beet tops
1½ cups nasturtium leaves
3 tablespoons chives, chopped
2 cucumbers, thinly sliced
½ cup radishes, thinly sliced
½ cup shallots, chopped

DIRECTIONS:

Combine all ingredients and toss lightly.

Add a salad dressing of your choice.

❖

SOUTHERN PECAN PIE

Number of Servings: 8

Preparation Time: 20–25 minutes

Cooking Time: 1 hour, 10 minutes

INGREDIENTS:

Pastry for a 10-inch pie
1 ¼ cups dark corn syrup
1 cup sugar
4 whole eggs
4 tablespoons melted butter
1 ½ cups pecans, chopped
1 teaspoon pure vanilla extract
2 tablespoons dark rum
Whipped cream

DIRECTIONS:

Preheat oven to 350 degrees. Roll out the pastry and line a 10-inch pie tin. Combine the corn syrup and sugar in a saucepan and bring to boil. Cook, stirring just until the sugar is dissolved. Beat the eggs in a mixing bowl and gradually add the sugar mixture, beating.

Add the remaining ingredients and pour mixture into the pie shell. Bake for 50 minutes to 1 hour, or until pie is set. Serve with whipped cream.

A PENNSYLVANIA GERMAN DINNER FROM THE EARLY AMERICAN LIFE SOCIETY

The first generation of settlers who came to be known as the Pennsylvania Germans immigrated to Pennsylvania in the seventeenth century from all over Europe. Years of social and religious insecurity made them hold to the soil. In their new home, the arts were renewed again and again with the succeeding migrations. Handsomely painted furniture, abstractly glazed sgraffito ware, and intricately woven

The walnut cupboard in the Pennsylvania German Room at Winterthur is filled with examples of lead-glazed red earthenware. Many of the sgraffito wares are signed and dated. These inscriptions provide contemporary views of religion, sex, marriage, and women's roles in the Pennsylvania German society. A plain-weave linen fabric, 1800, originating in the United States, covers the dining table.
Antiques shown include earthenware plates, 1820–1830, made in Pennsylvania; earthenware American castors, ca. 1850; pewter spoons, ca. 1710; horn-handled knives and forks, ca. 1850; American preserves jar, ca. 1820, used as a flower vase; Shenandoah earthenware covered dish, ca. 1890, from Virginia; New England earthenware pitcher, ca. 1825.
Other items include modern hexagonal-shaped glasses.

coverlets, hand towels, and other fabrics are significant parts of Winterthur's collection. They were acquired by Henry Francis du Pont in recognition of the Pennsylvania Germans' role in shaping the nation's artistic heritage. Many of today's practices and customs, including many associated with Christmas and Easter, hark back to the Pennsylvania Germans.

The Early American Society of Harrisburg, Pennsylvania, is the source of this hearty winter dinner from Pennsylvania German country. Baked Corn Pudding accompanies the traditional Chicken and Dumplings. Two rich and filling desserts —molasses-filled Shoo Fly Pie and Chocolate Cake—complete this informal country meal.

"Home cooking" is best served in a relaxed setting. For this meal, Pennsylvania German earthenware plates from the mid-1800s and pewter dating from the same period achieve the desired effect; the table is protected by a window-pane-check linen mattress cover. An earthenware bowl holds warm, fresh-from-the-oven egg twist-bread. Like the bowl, the pitcher and covered serving dish are dark-glazed earthenware.

Serve this stick-to-the-ribs meal with a good German beer, most appropriately a dark beer, or with warm mulled cider spiced with cloves and cinnamon sticks. Dessert can be accompanied by rich coffee, preferably a Viennese roast.

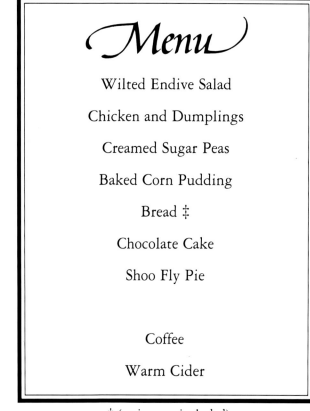

Menu

Wilted Endive Salad

Chicken and Dumplings

Creamed Sugar Peas

Baked Corn Pudding

Bread ‡

Chocolate Cake

Shoo Fly Pie

Coffee

Warm Cider

‡ (recipe not included)
Reprinted, with permission, from
The Early American Life Family Celebration Cookbook

PREPARATION TIP: PIE DOUGH

The secret to terrific pies is in the crust. Flaky, light piecrusts are memorable, whether they grace the dinner table on Thursday or at Thanksgiving.

There are a few keys to creating a good piecrust. First, be careful in measuring and mixing the ingredients. Large amounts of flour will make dough too dry and tough. With large amounts of shortening, dough will be too moist to handle easily. Soggy, gluelike dough results from too much water. To prevent problems, use a pastry cloth and rolling pin cover when rolling dough. These inexpensive and easy-to-use kitchen tools will cut down on the need for extra flour when rolling.

Second, handle pie dough as little as possible. Overhandling makes dough tough and results in a flat, heavy crust. Use only the amount of dough needed for one pie, and roll each crust separately. Refrigerated dough should be brought to room temperature before it is handled, cutting down on the amount of rolling necessary to form a crust.

Finally, be sure to preheat the oven before baking either filled or unfilled piecrusts. Unfilled shells will be lighter and airier if baked in a hot oven. Fillings will bake along with the piecrust, lessening the chance of overbrowning or sogginess.

WILTED ENDIVE (OR DANDELION) SALAD

Number of Servings: 6

Preparation Time: 15 minutes

Cooking Time: 20 minutes

INGREDIENTS:

6 pieces sugar-cured bacon
1 head endive, washed and shredded fine (dandelion greens can be substituted in season, mid-March to mid-May, late October to first freeze)
⅓ cup white distilled vinegar
¼ cup granulated sugar
½ teaspoon dry mustard
3 small spring onions, minced
1 hard-boiled egg, sliced

DIRECTIONS:

In a large frying pan fry bacon until crisp; remove and drain. Meanwhile, combine endive and onions. Over low heat, combine bacon drippings, vinegar, sugar, and dry mustard. Stir until sugar dissolves.

Add greens and onions to the vinegar mixture. Toss gently over low heat for 1 minute. Transfer to a bowl, crumble the bacon strips into the greens, and top with egg slices.

✣

CHICKEN AND DUMPLINGS

Number of Servings: 6

Preparation Time: 45 minutes

Cooking Time: 1 hour, 25 minutes

INGREDIENTS:

4 pounds chicken, cut into pieces
¼ cup flour
⅓ cup corn oil
1 large yellow cooking onion, sliced
½ cup dry white wine
6 cups chicken stock
1 celery stalk, cut into 1-inch pieces
1 bay leaf, medium size
¼ teaspoon ground sage
2 teaspoons salt
Black pepper to taste

Dumplings
2 cups flour
4 teaspoons baking powder
¾ teaspoon salt
2 tablespoons shortening
1 cup milk
¼ cup fresh parsley, chopped

DIRECTIONS:

Shake chicken pieces in flour in a plastic bag, 2 at a time, until thoroughly coated. In a deep frying pan or Dutch oven heat the oil, add chicken pieces, and fry, turning frequently, until golden. Remove chicken from the pan. Add sliced onion and sauté about 5 minutes, stirring frequently. When onion is soft and golden stir in white wine. Mix briskly. Return chicken pieces and add stock, celery, bay leaf, sage, salt, and pepper. Bring to a boil over high heat. Reduce to low, cover, and simmer for 45 minutes.

While chicken is simmering, prepare the dumpling batter.

Dumplings—Sift dry ingredients into a bowl. Cut in shortening. Add milk slowly, mixing with a fork until well blended. Add parsley. Batter should be lumpy.

When chicken finishes simmering, uncover and drop batter by spoonfuls into chicken. Cover tightly and simmer for 10 minutes without uncovering. Serve on one platter.

✤

CREAMED SUGAR PEAS

Number of Servings: 6

Preparation Time: 10 minutes

Cooking Time: 1 hour, 10 minutes

INGREDIENTS:

1 quart sugar peas
1 tablespoon butter
4 tablespoons heavy cream
1 teaspoon salt
⅓ teaspoon pepper

DIRECTIONS:

Wash peas thoroughly and remove stems. Simmer for 1 hour in enough water to cover. Melt butter in a small pan. Stir in heavy cream, salt, and pepper. Drain peas and immediately pour cream mixture over them; toss gently. Serve at once.

✤

BAKED CORN PUDDING

Number of Servings: 6

Preparation Time: 25 minutes

Cooking Time: 1 hour, 15 minutes

INGREDIENTS:

2 eggs
2 tablespoons granulated sugar
4 tablespoons flour
4 tablespoons butter, melted
1½ pints shoe peg corn
Salt to taste
1½ cups milk

DIRECTIONS:

Beat eggs, sugar and flour together to make a smooth paste. Pour in melted butter and mix until well blended. Stir in shoe peg corn and salt to taste. Mix until corn is well coated. Add milk and stir lightly. Pour into a greased 2-quart baking dish, cover, and bake at 400 degrees for 1 hour. Remove cover and bake an additional 15 minutes.

CHOCOLATE CAKE

Number of Servings: 12

Preparation Time: 25 minutes

Cooking Time: 30 minutes

INGREDIENTS:

2 cups flour
1 teaspoon baking soda
½ teaspoon salt
⅓ cup shortening or butter
1¼ cups granulated sugar
1 egg
3 ounces bitter chocolate
½ cup thick sour cream
¾ cup milk
1 teaspoon vanilla

Cream Cheese Frosting
8 ounces cream cheese
2 cups confectioners' sugar
½ teaspoon vanilla
2 tablespoons milk

DIRECTIONS:

Sift flour one time, add soda and salt, and sift together 3 more times. Cream butter or shortening with sugar until thoroughly blended. Add egg and beat well. Melt chocolate and add to egg and sugar mixture, blending until smooth. Add ¼ of flour mixture to chocolate mixture Add sour cream and mix thoroughly. Add remaining flour alternately with milk, beating well after each addition. Add vanilla. Pour mixture into greased 13" x 8" x 2" baking pan. Bake at 350 degrees for 30 minutes. When cool, top with cream cheese frosting.

Frosting—Cream the cheese, sugar, and vanilla together. When well blended, add milk to desired consistency. Spread thinly over cake.

SHOO FLY PIE

Number of Servings: 6

Preparation Time: 15 minutes

Cooking Time: 45 minutes

INGREDIENTS:

    1 cup molasses
    ⅓ cup hot water
    ½ teaspoon baking soda
    1 egg, well beaten
    1 8-inch pie shell, unbaked
    1 ½ cups flour
    ¼ cup shortening
    ¼ cup granulated sugar
    ⅔ cup dark brown sugar

DIRECTIONS:

Mix first 4 ingredients together until smooth. Pour into unbaked 8-inch pie shell. Mix rest of ingredients together with fork until crumbs form. Sprinkle on top of filling. Bake at 400 degrees for 45 minutes.

PAUL NEWMAN'S ITALIAN DINNER
AFTER THE RACES

*P*aul Newman's film career has spanned three decades and has included such modern classics as *The Hustler*, *Butch Cassidy and the Sundance Kid*, and *The Sting*. His auto-racing career earned him the U.S. championship at Atlanta in 1982. But, according to *Newman's Own Cookbook*, his "principal vocation is cooking." He has certainly proven his prowess in this area, producing Newman's Own All Natural and Industrial Strength Spaghetti Sauce, Newman's Own Salad Dressing, Newman's Own Lemonade, and Newman's Own Oldstyle Picture and Microwave Popcorn, as well as a cookbook of "simple, all natural, and imaginative" recipes.

Paul Newman's Italian dinner after the races combines at least two of his favorite pastimes. A stick-to-the-ribs dinner of homemade pasta with sauce; fresh tomato, mozzarella, and basil salad with dressing; crusty, fresh-baked *pain ordinaire*; and rich homemade spumoni is enough to satisfy even the hungriest race fan or pit-crew member.

A hearty menu like this one calls for an equally robust table setting. Woven checked placemats, thick glass goblets, and a bright floral centerpiece echo the informal tone of the dinnerware and convey more of Mr. Newman's preference for a simple, imaginative style. Individual votive candles shed light at each place so that diners can reread their race programs and view early photos of the day's events. What other atmosphere could be more conducive to relaxing after a long day at the races?

To accompany a dinner like this, nothing compares with a good, robust Italian red wine like an Amarone. A Spanish rioja or other full-bodied red will do the trick if an Italian wine is not available.

"Gaudy Dutch," early nineteenth-century Staffordshire earthenware featured in this dinner, was made in England as an imitation of colorful Imari porcelain. A great deal of this ware seems to have been exported to the United States. Much of it was found in Pennsylvania, giving rise to the belief that it was Pennsylvania German.
Other items shown include green glass goblets from Shield's, silverware from Reed & Barton, and a racing helmet and gloves courtesy of Alderman Nissan.

‡ (recipes not included)

PREPARATION TIPS: NEWMAN'S OWN ALL NATURAL SPAGHETTI SAUCE

Meat Sauce:	Brown ground beef, pour off fat and add sauce, and simmer gently for 5 minutes.
Seafood Sauce:	Add boiled shrimp, scallions, or clams to sauce.
Cream Sauce:	Add 1 cup heavy cream to 1 jar (32 ounces) of sauce for a Northern Italian light creamy tomato sauce.
Russian Dressing:	Combine 2 tablespoons mayonnaise and 2 tablespoons sauce and mix well.
Topping:	Meatloaf—top your favorite meatloaf recipe with sauce and bake. Omelet—top a cheese-and-parsley omelet with sauce. Garnish with parsley and grated Parmesan. Pasta—use sauce or any of the above sauce variations on tortellini, ravioli, fettucine, linguine, etc.

Rice:	Add sautéed onions, red and green peppers, and sauce to cooked rice.
Quick Pizza:	Top a toasted English muffin with sauce and grated mozzarella and toast until bubbly in toaster oven. On any pizza, add sauce for extra flavor.

From *Newman's Own 22 Favorite Recipes*, Newman's Own, Inc., 1985.

HOMEMADE PASTA

Number of Servings: 10

Preparation Time: 1 hour

Cooking Time: 5 minutes

INGREDIENTS:

6 cups flour
2½ tablespoons salt
4 eggs
⅔ cup water

DIRECTIONS:

Mix flour and salt. Beat eggs and add slowly to flour mixture. Mix until well incorporated. Add water in a slow steady stream to make a soft, well formed, but not sticky, dough. Cover dough and set aside for 30 minutes. Turn out on a lightly floured board. Knead dough until smooth and elastic. Divide dough into 8 pieces, shape each into a long roll, and flatten with a rolling pin to a width slightly smaller than the width of your pasta machine. Follow machine directions for spaghetti.

Allow to dry, then cook for 5 minutes in boiling water. Fresh pasta can be stored in a tightly covered container.

Serve with Newman's Own All Natural Spaghetti Sauce.

HOMEMADE FRENCH BREAD

Yield: 1 loaf

Preparation Time: 5 hours

Cooking Time: 40 minutes

INGREDIENTS:

1 cup lukewarm water
1½ teaspoons salt

1 cake compressed yeast
3½ to 3¾ cups flour, sifted

Pour lukewarm water over the salt and crumbled yeast. Add 2 cups of the flour and beat well. Add enough flour to make a soft dough or until the dough begins to clean the sides of the bowl and can be easily handled.

Turn onto a floured board and knead dough until smooth and elastic to the touch, approximately 10 to 12 minutes. Shape dough into a ball and place in a greased bowl; cover and allow to rise in a warm place (80 to 85 degrees) until double the bulk—about 2 hours or longer. An impression should remain when a finger is pressed deep in the side of the dough.

Turn dough out onto a lightly floured board and knead briefly. Shape into a long rope, approximately the same length as the bread mold. Grease mold lightly and arrange dough in mold. Cover loosely with a clean, dry kitchen towel and let rise in a warm place until double in bulk, about 1 hour. Remove towel and give dough 3 parallel slices across the top with a sharp knife. Bake in preheated oven for 40 minutes at 400 degrees, turning and brushing with cold water at 10-minute intervals.

✤

SPUMONI

Number of Servings: 4
Preparation Time: 20 minutes
Cooking Time: 3 minutes
Freezing: 2 hours

INGREDIENTS:

¾ cup water
10 tablespoons sugar
½-inch piece of vanilla bean
5 egg yolks
2 egg whites
¼ teaspoon salt
1 cup whipped cream
1 teaspoon candied angelica
1 teaspoon citron, finely chopped
1 teaspoon cherries, finely chopped
2 tablespoons almonds, finely blanched
1 teaspoon candied lemon peel, finely chopped
1 teaspoon candied orange peel, finely chopped

DIRECTIONS:

Make a syrup by boiling the water, 5 tablespoons sugar, and the vanilla bean for 3 minutes. Discard the vanilla bean and pour the syrup very slowly over 5 well-beaten egg yolks. Beat briskly and constantly to prevent the yolks from curdling. In another bowl, beat the egg whites and salt until egg whites are stiff. Gradually beat 5 tablespoons sugar, 1 tablespoon at a time, alternately with 1 cup whipped cream. Combine the egg-white mixture gradually with the egg-yolk mixture, beating, and fold in candied angelica, citron, cherries, almonds, and candied lemon and orange peel. Turn the cream into a spumoni mold, or any 1-quart mold, and freeze.

MALCOLM FORBES'S "I TOLD YOU I COULD COOK" DINNER

Military medals and china bearing the likenesses of our forefathers dignify Malcolm Forbes's dinner table; a soldier stands sentry over the elegant meal. Long admired for his business acumen, Mr. Forbes has also won wide recognition as a collector. His celebrated collection of jeweled and enameled Fabergé eggs, made originally for the czars of Russia, is the world's finest, larger even than that of the Hermitage Museum in Leningrad. No less colorful is his fleet of hot-air balloons, which, with the sunlight behind them, glisten like gems in the sky.

Of all Mr. Forbes's many collections, which range from Victorian paintings to toy boats, his assemblage of military miniatures is said to be his favorite. He calls his legions of model soldiers, exhibited in his museum in Tangiers, the "largest standing army in northern Africa."

Mr. Forbes says "I told you I could cook" with a lavish and elegant dinner. And he says it with an admirable menu featuring Butterflied Leg of Lamb.

Serve this elegant dinner with an equally elegant wine. A dry red wine, such as a Bordeaux, will go well with the lamb. A very dry Spanish sherry is nice with—or in —the soup. If desired, dessert should be accompanied by a light white wine that will complement its sweetness without overpowering it.

The fine French porcelain, ca. 1817, is decorated with stipple-painted portraits in black of American statesmen or military heroes of the Battle of 1812. The ovoid glassware with copper wheel-engraved decoration was made in Bohemia, Germany, ca. 1775. The cabriole armchairs, ca. 1810, are from Philadelphia.
Complementing the tableware are American campaign medals and decorations for the serious collector to peruse. The papier mâché soldier is from a private collection.

Menu

Potato & Watercress Soup

Butterflied Leg of Lamb

Country Creamed Potatoes

Peas and Onions ‡

Strawberry Glacé

Château Margaux 1975

‡ (recipe not included)

PREPARATION TIPS: LAMB

The key to superb lamb is to cook it to perfection—not too rare, not too well done, just cooked until pink and still tender. This method of broiling butterflied leg of lamb makes the cooking time quick and the preparation relatively easy. Yet the finished product is an elegant entrée for a special meal.

Marinating gives lamb its special flavor and adds to its tenderness. It tenderizes the meat, making for a shorter cooking time. Although the recipe calls for 4 hours marinating time, no harm will be done if the lamb soaks a bit longer. Make the marinade at your convenience the morning or early afternoon that you intend to serve the meal.

POTATO & WATERCRESS SOUP

Number of Servings: 6

Preparation Time: 10 minutes

Cooking Time: 25 minutes

INGREDIENTS:

3 tablespoons chicken fat or butter
6 large potatoes
3 medium-size onions
3 cups water
Salt and black pepper
3 bunches watercress
1½ cups milk
1½ cups light cream

DIRECTIONS:

Dissolve fat in a heavy, deep kettle. Add potatoes and onions, peeled and finely chopped. Add the water, salt, and pepper. Cover the pot and cook very slowly until the vegetables are mushy. Add the stalks and leaves of the watercress; cover and cook another minute. Rub through a fine strainer, then add the milk and the cream. Add more seasoning if necessary. Reheat; do not boil.

BUTTERFLIED LEG OF LAMB

Number of Servings: 6

Preparation Time: 20 minutes, plus 4 hours marinating time

Cooking Time: 20 minutes

INGREDIENTS:

Leg of lamb (5 to 6 pounds)
½ cup Dijon mustard
2 tablespoons soy sauce
½ teaspoon dried ginger
1 garlic clove, minced
3 tablespoons olive oil
1 teaspoon dried rosemary

DIRECTIONS:

Bone leg of lamb and split it open to resemble a butterfly. Combine remaining ingredients, and marinate lamb in mixture for 4 hours—turning frequently. Broil each side for 10 minutes, or until meat is pink in center. Slice at a diagonal and serve.

COUNTRY CREAMED POTATOES

Number of Servings: 6

Preparation Time: 10 minutes

Cooking Time: 20–25 minutes

INGREDIENTS:

3 cups cooked potatoes, diced
1½ cups light cream
2 tablespoons butter
1 tablespoon minced onion
½ teaspoon salt
½ teaspoon pepper
Parsley, minced

DIRECTIONS:

Place diced cooked potatoes in a saucepan. Add cream, butter, onion, salt, and pepper. Cover and simmer over low heat for 20 to 25 minutes, or until slightly thickened, stirring occasionally. Sprinkle with parsley and serve.

STRAWBERRY GLACÉ

Number of Servings: 6

Preparation Time: 10 minutes

Cooking Time: 20 minutes

Freezing Time: 3–4 hours

INGREDIENTS:

1 cup sugar
1 cup water
2 cups strawberries, fresh or frozen
4 egg yolks
2 cups light cream, scalded
2 cups heavy cream, whipped
Few mint sprigs

DIRECTIONS:

Combine ½ cup sugar and the water in a saucepan. Cook until syrupy, about 5 minutes. Add the strawberries, cook another 5 minutes, and force syrup through a sieve. Set aside. Beat the egg yolks and remaining sugar in the top of a double boiler. Gradually add the light cream, stirring steadily. Place over hot water and cook, stirring constantly until thick. Strain. Add to strawberry syrup. Cool. Fold in the whipped cream. Pour the mixture into a 2-quart soufflé dish. Place in the freezing compartment of refrigerator and freeze for 3–4 hours. Remove from refrigerator and let set out for 10 minutes, then place soufflé dish into a larger pan of hot water for a few minutes to loosen the edges of the glacé. Spoon into individual glass serving bowls and garnish with a mint sprig.

MARIO BUATTA'S DINNER BEFORE THE THEATER

*D*ubbed the "Prince of Chintz" for his magical use of flowery fabrics, Mr. Buatta is credited with bringing into fashion the "undecorated look," a balance of comfort and elegance that creates a lovely, timeless, livable environment. His trademarks? His eclectic combinations of the old and the new; his use of color, especially to achieve painterly hued backgrounds; and his creative juxtapositions of patterns, designs, and small "treasures" throughout an environment. His association with Winterthur dates back to 1981, when he was commissioned to design the galleries that would house the fledgling Winterthur Reproduction Collection.

Mr. Buatta's style is evident in both the setting of and menu for this elegant dinner before the theater. Winterthur's Chinese Parlor holds a table set to do this dinner proud, a table on which antiques and contemporary objects are displayed with great flair and attention to detail. The overall effect is elegant but comfortable, exotic and lush yet intimate.

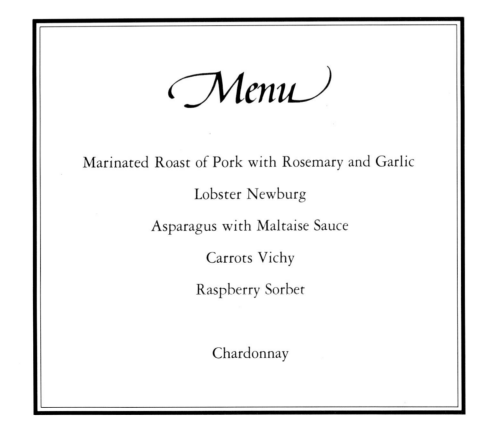

Menu

Marinated Roast of Pork with Rosemary and Garlic

Lobster Newburg

Asparagus with Maltaise Sauce

Carrots Vichy

Raspberry Sorbet

Chardonnay

Like the dinner table, the menu incorporates subtle paradoxes. Old favorites are presented from a new angle, à la Buatta, giving them extra excitement and flavor. The sumptuous menu is highlighted by Roast Pork marinated in raspberry vinegar, garlic, and rosemary; Asparagus with Maltaise Sauce (an orange-flavored hollandaise); and Lobster Newburg.

Mr. Buatta suggests a full-bodied white wine to accompany the meal. Chardonnay might be the perfect companion for both the pork and the lobster.

PREPARATION TIPS: HOLLANDAISE SAUCE

There is no such thing as a low-calorie hollandaise sauce. But then without all that butter and all those eggs, hollandaise sauce would not be what it is—the finishing touch for even the plainest steamed vegetables, the touch of glamour that makes any meal magical.

Like other hot egg sauces, hollandaise sauce has its quirks. It is not difficult to make, if cooked slowly and with care. Most cookbooks recommend cooking the sauce over hot, not boiling, water, although those written by professional chefs generally say that cooking over direct heat is more efficient. However, amateur chefs are wise to take the safe route and use a double boiler for preparing the hollandaise.

When cooking, be sure to whisk constantly and add the butter slowly until the hollandaise is thick enough that the whisk leaves marks in the sauce. The sauce may sit in a warm place for half an hour before it is used. At this point it can also be cooled and frozen for later, although it loses some of its consistency in thawing.

Hollandaise sauce can recover from any number of maladies, even after it appears to be irreparably damaged. Thin, foamy sauce is too cold. Add a little hot water and beat the sauce over hot water until it thickens. Curdled sauce can be saved by adjusting the cooking temperature and whisking until the sauce is smooth.

In the Chinese Parlor at Winterthur the hand-painted wall covering, ca. 1770, depicting life in a Chinese village, is evidence of the Western world's fascination with the Orient—an interest that began in the seventeenth century and continues undiminished today. The lovely figurines on the table, ca. 1850, are also from China and possibly represent a mandarin and his wife. They are made of plaster, wood, and stone and have heads attached with weighted rods inserted into hollow bodies to allow a nodding motion.

Antiques shown include Chinese porcelain, ca. 1785; lead glass champagne glasses, ca. 1800; silver salt dishes, ca. 1846, made by Robert and William Wilson of Philadelphia; silver salt spoons, ca. 1840, made by Garrett Eoff of New York. Other items shown include modern jade figurines and a serving bell of silver.

Marinated Roast of Pork with Rosemary and Garlic

Number of Servings: 4–6

Preparation Time: 10 minutes, plus 2 hours marinating time

Cooking Time: 1½–1¾ hours

INGREDIENTS:

Boneless pork roast (3–4 pounds)
⅓ cup raspberry vinegar
⅓ cup vegetable oil
¾ teaspoon garlic powder
1 garlic clove, crushed
½ teaspoon Adobo powder (salt, garlic, oregano, black pepper, MSG)
2 tablespoons rosemary leaves
¼ teaspoon pepper, freshly cracked

DIRECTIONS:

Place roast into a loaf pan. Pour vinegar and oil over the roast. Sprinkle the remaining ingredients over the meat. Cover with plastic wrap and place in refrigerator for 2 hours, turning meat over once. Remove from refrigerator and place meat onto a roasting pan, reserving all liquid. Bake at 350 degrees for 1½ to 1¾ hours, basting occasionally with marinade.

Lobster Newburg

Number of Servings: 4–6

Preparation Time: 50–60 minutes

Cooking Time: 25–30 minutes

INGREDIENTS:

¾ pound butter
4 ounces flour
1 quart milk, hot
Fresh lobster (3 to 4 pounds), cleaned and cut into bite-sized pieces
1 teaspoon paprika
1 ounce sherry wine
Salt
Lemon wedges
Parsley
Toast points

DIRECTIONS:

Melt ½ pound of butter in a heavy sauce pot and add the flour to make a roux, stirring constantly. Cook for 8 to 10 minutes, but do not brown. Pour in the scalded milk and stir sauce until thickened and smooth. Sauté the lobster in the remaining ¼ pound of butter for about 10 minutes. Add paprika to the lobster. Add the lobster to the sauce, add the wine, and season lightly with salt. Garnish with lemon wedges and fresh parsley. Serve on toast points.

ASPARAGUS WITH MALTAISE SAUCE

Number of Servings: 4

Preparation Time: 10 minutes, plus 4 hours freezing time

Cooking Time: 5–10 minutes

INGREDIENTS:

2 cups hollandaise sauce, prepared and still warm
⅓ cup orange juice
1 teaspoon orange peel, finely grated
Steamed asparagus spears (1½ to 2 pounds)

DIRECTIONS:

In a small saucepan, over medium heat, combine the hollandaise sauce with the orange juice and peel, beating constantly until smooth. Serve warm over asparagus spears. Garnish with additional orange peel or with sliced oranges.

CARROTS VICHY

Number of Servings: 4

Preparation Time: 10 minutes

Cooking Time: 20 minutes

INGREDIENTS:

1 pound even-sized carrots
⅔ cup water
2 tablespoons butter
Salt to taste
Black pepper, freshly cracked, to taste
1 teaspoon sugar
Fresh parsley, chopped

DIRECTIONS:

Wash the carrots; cut them into very thin rounds. Place the rounds in a saucepan with water, butter, seasoning, and sugar. Press a piece of buttered wax paper down onto the carrots, cover with a lid, and cook gently for about 20 minutes, until tender. The liquid should disappear, and the carrots will begin to cook gently in the butter and become lightly browned. Sprinkle with parsley and more freshly cracked black pepper.

RASPBERRY SORBET

Number of Servings: 6
Preparation Time: 25 minutes
Cooking Time: 5 minutes
Freezing Time: 4 hours

INGREDIENTS:

1 ½ cups sugar
½ cup water
½ cup kirsch
2 cups rinsed raspberries, pureed
Juice of 1 large lemon
2 egg whites
2 tablespoons brandy
Whipped cream

DIRECTIONS:

Mix together sugar, water, and kirsch, and stir the mixture over very low heat until the sugar is dissolved. Boil the mixture steadily for 5 minutes. Remove it from the heat, and add the raspberries and unstrained lemon juice. Cool the mixture thoroughly. Stir in the stiffly beaten egg whites and add the brandy. Freeze mixture for at least 4 hours. To serve, use an ice cream scoop to make balls of sorbet. Place in individual frosted glasses with a touch of whipped cream.

A FORMAL DINNER
WITH JAY E. CANTOR

As the expert in American painting at the acclaimed auction house Christie's in New York, Jay Cantor is a connoisseur in every sense of the word. He knows his subjects thoroughly, often recognizing quality in works others have deemed unexceptional. He has developed a "sixth sense" about works of art, as well as an unerring eye. In addition to his responsibilities at Christie's, he finds time for research and writing. His most recent publication is *Winterthur*, published by Harry N. Abrams, Inc.

Mr. Cantor's attention to quality is as much evident in his entertaining as it is in his professional work; he is always looking for "the best," whether it be a superb work of art or a perfectly prepared meal. Often called on to entertain clients and colleagues, Mr. Cantor creates dinners that are as spectacular as some of the record-breaking sales he is responsible for.

This formal dinner menu features several unique dishes using ingredients that have become popular only recently in the United States. Each dish represents an interesting and fresh approach to the way in which color, texture, and taste may be combined in foods.

A colorful chilled Beet Salad served on tender Bibb lettuce starts the meal. The salad is followed by a rich Spinach Leek Soup, which may be served hot or cold. The centerpiece of the menu, grilled Veal Chops seasoned with mustard, is served with Wild Rice, enhanced by carrots, Shitake Mushrooms, and molded Timbales of Green Beans and Peas. A dramatic cold Cassis Soufflé garnished with delicate crystallized violets is the pièce de résistance.

Neoclassical accents help create a stately setting for this special dinner party. Antique footed serving dishes, "urn" vases, and pressed-glass salts all evoke images of ancient Greece and Rome. An opulent arrangement of roses, snapdragons, gladioli, and spiky chrysanthemums fill a Chinese export porcelain bowl decorated with the American eagle.

A light but spicy wine is a fine accompaniment for this meal. A dry blush, such as a Cabernet Blanc, is appropriate. Serve the soufflé with extra crème de cassis for pouring, as well as champagne for drinking.

Menu

Beet Salad with Mustard Vinaigrette

Spinach Leek Soup

Veal Chops Dijon

Wild Rice with Shitake Mushrooms

Timbales of Green Beans and Peas

Cassis Soufflé

Cabernet Blanc

Champagne

The Georgia Dining Room at Winterthur is from the Samuel Rockwell mansion, built ca. 1837 in Milledgeville, Georgia. The room's mahogany extension dining table of 1810– 1819 bears the stamp of the French émigré cabinetmaker Charles-Honoré Lannuier (working 1803–1819). Around the table is a set of painted Klismos-type side chairs, characterized by broad slat backs combined with sabre-shaped front and rear legs, made in New York or Philadelphia, 1810–1825.

Antiques shown include "Fitzhugh" pattern Chinese porcelain, ca. 1775; a set of Rockingham porcelain vases, ca. 1815, from England; champagne glasses, ca. 1800; free-blown and molded glass decanters, ca. 1800, from Pittsburgh; a silver dish cross, ca. 1820, made by Gerardus Boyce of New York; a silver covered bowl on a stand, ca. 1817, the silver shell-shaped salts, ca. 1846, made by R. & W. Wilson of Philadelphia; and eighteenth-century silverware. The Winterthur reproduction stemware "Brandywine," adapted from an eighteenth-century goblet in the Flock Room, is perfect for Cabernet Blanc.

PREPARATION TIPS: VEAL

Veal is the meat of very young beef cattle, usually under six months old. It has recently become popular in the United States because, like chicken, veal is much lower in fat and cholesterol than red meat.

Very young veal is light pink in color, sometimes ranging to almost white. The deeper pink the meat, the older the calf from which it was taken and the more likely it will be tough.

Because veal is so low in fat it cooks rapidly and can become very tough. Take precautions by cooking veal in a slow oven; if grilling or sautéing, keep it away from high heat. Thick veal chops are most appropriate for grilling because they cook less quickly than thinly sliced cutlets or medallions of meat.

To tenderize veal cutlets, soak them in milk and pound before cooking. This process breaks down much of the tough tissue, making the cutlets less stringy and chewy.

Veal is excellent when prepared with lemon or some other citrus fruit, or with Madeira, marsala, or other wine. It is a versatile meat, well worth the expense and the care needed to cook it.

BEET SALAD WITH MUSTARD VINAIGRETTE

Number of Servings: 6

Preparation Time: 15 minutes

Cooking Time: 25 minutes

INGREDIENTS:

4 cups fresh cooked beets, cold
1 tablespoon cider vinegar
2 tablespoons lemon juice
2 teaspoons sugar
¼ cup Dijon mustard
½ cup olive oil
1 tablespoon parsley, finely chopped
3 tablespoons fresh dill, finely chopped
Salt and pepper
Bibb or Boston lettuce
2 hard-boiled eggs, chopped
Dill sprigs

DIRECTIONS:

Cut beets into fine matchsticks. Combine vinegar, lemon juice, and sugar in a jar. Add mustard and stir. Add olive oil, parsley, chopped dill, and salt and pepper. Cover and shake vigorously. Pour over beets. Arrange tender lettuce such as Bibb or Boston on individual plates, add beets, and garnish with chopped hard-boiled eggs and sprigs of dill. (Salad is better if served slightly chilled.)

SPINACH LEEK SOUP

Number of Servings: 6

Preparation Time: 15 minutes

Cooking Time: 45 minutes

INGREDIENTS:

1 onion, sliced
2 leeks, sliced
¼ cup butter
2 Idaho potatoes, cubed
¾ package of spinach, chopped
4 or 5 leaves Boston lettuce, chopped
Salt and pepper
2 beef bouillon cubes
4 cups boiling water

DIRECTIONS:

In a covered casserole, sauté onions and leeks in butter until soft. Add potatoes and continue to cook until slightly browned. Add spinach and lettuce to casserole; cover and wilt. Season with salt and pepper and cover vegetables with boiling water. Add bouillon cubes and simmer over low heat for 25 minutes. Cool slightly. Put through a sieve or food processor. Additional water may be added to thin soup, if desired. May be served cold (soup is better cold if slightly thinned).

❖

VEAL CHOPS DIJON

Number of Servings: 6

Preparation Time: 15 minutes

Cooking Time: 15 minutes

INGREDIENTS:

4 tablespoons unsalted butter, melted
1 ½ tablespoons Dijon mustard
1 shallot, minced
1 tablespoon parsley, chopped
1 tablespoon tarragon
1 tablespoon chives, chopped
12 veal chops
Fresh ground pepper

DIRECTIONS:

Combine first 6 ingredients. Brush chops with butter mixture. Place chops over hot coals. Turn them every couple of minutes, brushing with butter mixture before turning. Cook chops 10 to 15 minutes, depending on their thickness. Pepper to taste. If preparing chops under a broiler, cook them 12 to 15 minutes, turning every 4 or 5 minutes and basting as before.

❖

Wild Rice with Shitake Mushrooms

Number of Servings: 6

Preparation Time: 15 minutes, plus 30 minutes for soaking

Cooking Time: 1 hour, 25 minutes

INGREDIENTS:

1 ounce dried shitake mushrooms
1 cup warm water
2 tablespoons shallots, chopped
2 tablespoons sweet butter
2 cups carrots, thinly sliced
8 ounces raw wild rice
3 cups water or chicken stock
Salt and pepper to taste
Parsley

DIRECTIONS:

Soak mushrooms for 30 minutes. Drain through a sieve lined with cheesecloth or a paper towel. Reserve liquid. Cut off tough stems and discard. Cut mushrooms into slivers. In a heavy saucepan, sauté the shallots in butter until soft. Add carrots and mushrooms and coat with butter. Add rice and stir. Add water or stock and mushroom liquid, salt, and pepper. Heat to a simmer, cover, and place in preheated 350-degree oven. Cook for 1 hour and 15 minutes, until liquid is absorbed and rice is fluffy. Remove from oven and set aside for 15 minutes. Put into serving bowl and fluff with fork. Garnish with parsley.

❖

Timbales of Green Beans and Peas

Number of Servings: 6

Preparation Time: 20 minutes

Cooking Time: 40 minutes

INGREDIENTS:

1 pound green beans
1 cup cooked peas
1 shallot, chopped
4 tablespoons butter, plus additional
    butter for wax paper and molds
Salt and pepper to taste
3 eggs
¾ cup cream
1 teaspoon nutmeg
Parsley, minced, for garnish

DIRECTIONS:

Cook grean beans 5 minutes in boiling salted water, drain, trim, and chop. Steam beans together with peas and chopped shallot for 8 minutes in butter in a covered skillet. Cool slightly. Puree and add salt and pepper to taste. Beat eggs and cream lightly; add nutmeg, salt, and pepper. Combine with bean/pea puree.

Butter 6 timbale molds (¾ cup each), fill, and cover with buttered rounds of wax paper. Place in pan. Fill pan with water ⅔ up sides of the molds. Bake in a 350-degree oven for 25 minutes. Remove pan from oven and molds from the pan. Let the molds stand 5 minutes. Remove wax paper and invert molds on serving plate. Garnish with parsley.

❖

Cassis Soufflé

INGREDIENTS:

- 1 package, plus 1 teaspoon unflavored gelatin
- ¼ cup warm water
- Butter
- 4 egg yolks
- ½ cup sugar
- ⅛ teaspoon salt
- 1¼ cups crème de cassis
- 1 cup heavy cream, whipped
- 6 egg whites
- Red food coloring (optional)
- Crystallized violets

DIRECTIONS:

Sprinkle gelatin over warm water and soften. Prepare a soufflé dish with an aluminum-foil collar. Butter entire surface of inner mold, including the collar. Secure collar with a string so collar extends above the edge of the dish.

Put egg yolks, sugar, salt, and softened gelatin in top of double boiler and set over hot water on medium heat. Beat with wire whisk. Do not allow mixture to boil. When thick and creamy, remove from heat and beat in cassis.

Place the custard in a large bowl and chill until it starts to thicken (about 3 hours), stirring occasionally to ensure even thickening.

At this point, if a pink color is desired, add a scant drop of red food coloring. In a separate bowl, beat egg whites until stiff but not dry. Add ⅓ of the egg whites to cassis custard. Combine. Then add remaining egg whites and whipped cream, being careful not to overmix. Spoon or pour into the prepared soufflé dish and chill for several hours. May be prepared the day before and chilled overnight. Remove the aluminum-foil collar and garnish with crystallized violets. Additional crème de cassis may be served.

CLEMENT E. CONGER'S DINNER WITH GEORGE WASHINGTON

s curator of the State Department's Diplomatic Reception Rooms, Clement E. Conger has amassed almost singlehandedly one of the world's most important collections of early American decorative arts. When the rooms first opened twenty-six years ago, Mr. Conger was deputy chief of protocol and knew little about American antiques. Since then—like Henry Francis du Pont, self-taught and determined—Mr. Conger has become recognized as one of this country's preeminent authorities on early American furniture and art objects.

Showcases of American culture and craftsmanship, the Diplomatic Reception Rooms are first and foremost an area in which to entertain, a hospitable environment for gracious gatherings. A recent formal dinner to announce the establishment of an endowment fund saluted George Washington as one of America's great diplomats. The lavish eighteenth-century menu, adapted to modern taste, was as impressive as the dinner's majestic surroundings.

Several of the eighteenth-century favorites, including Roast Duckling, Poached Apples, Chestnuts, and Wild Rice, have been brought up to date by spices and sauces used in the style of the twentieth century. Essence of Tomato Soup, Watercress and Lettuce Salad, and Charlotte Russe with Brandied Peach Halves round out the meal.

Appropriately, the setting at Winterthur for this dinner focuses on Gilbert Stuart's portrait of Washington displayed in the Du Pont Dining Room.

Several wines are recommended to accompany this menu: a Meursault to begin the meal, followed by a Bordeaux and champagne, and cognac after dinner. For those who prefer a full-bodied red wine, pinot chardonnay would be an appropriate alternative.

Menu

Crab Mornay, Vol-au-Vent

Essence of Tomato Soup

Cheddar Sesame Crisps

Watercress and Lettuce Salad

Roast Duckling with Calvados Sauce

Poached Apple Slices with Chestnut Puree

Wild Rice and Mushroom Ring with Snap Beans

Charlotte Russe with Brandied Peach Halves

Meursault Domaine Joseph Matrot

Château Duhart-Milon-Rothschild Pauillas 1978

Dom Pérignon 1973

Demitasse

The Du Pont Dining Room contains a set of twelve New York mahogany arm and side chairs originally owned by Victor Marie du Pont, 1767–1827. Above the fireplace hangs an oil portrait of George Washington, 1795–1796, by Gilbert Stuart. The cupboards that flank the fireplace are filled with Chinese export porcelain decorated with a variation of the Great Seal of the United States.

Antiques shown include silver candlesticks, ca. 1771, made by John Carter; silver forks, ca. 1795, made by Thomas Harland of Norwich, Connecticut; silver pistol-handled knives, ca. 1828, from Baltimore, Maryland; Spode porcelain dinnerware, ca. 1805, from Staffordshire, England; rose-colored glass tumblers, ca. 1830; wine and water glasses, ca. 1830, engraved with the emblem of the Society of the Cincinnati; and silver cake baskets, ca. 1810.

Other objects include modern fruit-shaped enamel boxes.

Duckling has a reputation for being very fatty and rich. Therefore, before roasting, pierce the skin of the duckling in several places to allow fat to drain as it is rendered during cooking. Start roasting with the oven very hot to draw out fat and achieve a crisp dark skin. Once the duckling is well on its way to cooking, lower the oven and continue roasting more slowly.

If serving stuffing with the duckling, prepare it in a separate dish. Stuffing made in the bird will absorb a great deal of fat and be very greasy. If desired, fill the duckling with bread to absorb grease, to be discarded after cooking. With all stuffed fowl be sure to allow additional roasting time, up to 5 minutes per pound.

Do not underestimate the amount of duckling to be served to each guest. Plan on about 1 to 1½ pounds of meat for each person before cooking. And, although this meat is rich, it is extremely flavorful; have on hand enough to furnish seconds for the hearty eater.

CRAB MORNAY, VOL-AU-VENT

Number of Servings: 10

Preparation Time: 10 minutes

Cooking Time: 15 minutes

INGREDIENTS:

1 cup scallions, finely chopped
4 tablespoons butter
2 tablespoons flour
1 pint heavy cream
½ pound Jarlsberg cheese, finely grated
½ cup parsley, minced
2 tablespoons sherry
Hot pepper sauce and salt to taste
1 pound crabmeat
10 puff-pastry shells
Parsley sprigs

DIRECTIONS:

Sauté scallions in butter and add flour. Cook for 3 minutes over medium heat, without browning. Add cream and cheese, mixing well. Add parsley, sherry, hot pepper sauce, and salt. Simmer for 10 minutes on low heat, then gently fold into the crabmeat with a rubber spatula. Pour the Crab Mornay into prepared puff-pastry shells. Serve hot. Garnish with fresh parsley sprigs. Puff-pastry shells can be purchased frozen at the grocery store.

ESSENCE OF TOMATO SOUP

Number of Servings: 10

Preparation Time: 20 minutes

Cooking Time: 1 hour, 45 minutes

INGREDIENTS:

1 tablespoon onion, finely chopped
5 tablespoons butter
2 28-ounce cans whole tomatoes, chopped
6 fresh tomatoes, chopped
1 tablespoon fresh garlic, pressed
2½ cups beef consommé
2½ cups tomato juice
1 16-ounce can tomato sauce
¼ cup sugar
Salt, cayenne, and ground white pepper to taste

DIRECTIONS:

In large saucepan, sauté onion in butter until golden brown. Add chopped tomatoes and garlic and sauté on high heat, 2 to 3 minutes. Add beef consommé and tomato juice and bring to a boil. Add tomato sauce, sugar, salt, cayenne, and white pepper. Let simmer over low heat for 1 hour, 30 minutes. Before serving, strain through fine mesh strainer. Serve hot.

✤

CHEDDAR SESAME CRISPS

Yield: 2½ dozen

Preparation Time: 5—10 minutes

Cooking Time: 12—15 minutes

INGREDIENTS:

1 pound sharp cheddar cheese, grated
½ pound butter
3 tablespoons bacon fat
2 cups flour
½ teaspoon garlic salt
up to 30 drops hot pepper sauce
up to 10 drops Worcestershire sauce
6 tablespoons sesame seeds, toasted

DIRECTIONS:

Mix all ingredients together thoroughly. With hands, shape dough into long, smooth roll 2 inches in diameter. Wrap in waxed paper and chill in refrigerator until firm enough to slice easily. When ready to bake, slice into desired thickness. Bake on a cookie sheet at 425 degrees for 12 to 15 minutes. Cool on wire rack.

✤

ROAST DUCKLING
WITH CALVADOS SAUCE

Number of Servings: 8–10

Preparation Time: 5–10 minutes

Cooking Time: 2 hours, 30 minutes

INGREDIENTS:

    2 ducklings (4- to 5-pounds each), cleaned and
      prepared for roasting
    Salt and pepper to taste

DIRECTIONS:

Preheat oven to 400 degrees. Sprinkle the ducklings inside and out with salt and pepper to taste, and truss them with string. Place the ducklings on their sides in a roasting pan and bake for 30 minutes, basting occasionally. Drain excess fat from pan and repeat procedure for other side of ducklings, baking for 30 minutes. Drain excess fat once again, and place ducklings breast side up. Continue roasting for 1 hour to 1 hour and 30 minutes at 350 degrees, pouring off fat as it accumulates in the pan. The ducklings are done when they are taken from oven and the liquid runs clear. Serve with Calvados Sauce.

CALVADOS SAUCE

Yield: 2 cups

Preparation Time: 8–10 minutes

Cooking Time: 40–45 minutes

INGREDIENTS:

    7 tablespoons butter
    1 ounce shallots, minced
    ⅓ cup white wine
    ½ cup calvados (brandy made from apples, instead of
      the traditional grapes)
    3 cups duck or chicken stock
    3 tablespoons flour

DIRECTIONS:

Sauté shallots in 4 tablespoons of butter until they are transparent. Add the white wine and reduce over medium-high heat until almost dry. Add ¼ cup calvados and reduce again. Add stock and simmer 15 to 20 minutes in another saucepan. Make a roux by browning flour in remaining butter (use more butter if needed). Add calvados mixture to roux gradually, whisking constantly. Strain through a fine sieve. Flambé the remaining calvados and add to the sauce.

POACHED APPLE SLICES
WITH CHESTNUT PUREE

Number of Servings: 8–10

Preparation Time: 5–10 minutes

Cooking Time: 8–9 minutes

INGREDIENTS:

4 to 5 cooking apples, 2 thick slices cut from middle,
    peel left intact and cored
Water to cover
6 whole cloves
Few strips of lemon peel
1 2-inch stick of cinnamon
¼ cup sugar

DIRECTIONS:

Prepare apples and place in large saucepan. Cover with water and add cloves, lemon peel, cinnamon, and sugar. Simmer syrup for 5 minutes. Cook until tender but not mushy, 3 to 4 minutes. Use as a garnish with roast duckling. Serve with Chestnut Puree.

❖

CHESTNUT PUREE

Yield: 1 ½ cups

Preparation Time: 20–30 minutes

Cooking Time: 20–25 minutes

INGREDIENTS:

2 pounds chestnuts
1 quart milk
5 small pieces of celery
1 small bay leaf
Salt and pepper to taste
3 tablespoons butter

DIRECTIONS:

Make slits in the flat sides of each chestnut. Place on a shallow baking sheet and bake in a very hot oven, between 450 and 500 degrees, for 10 minutes, or until the shells start to curl back. Shell and peel the chestnuts while they are still hot.

Mix together milk, celery, and bay leaf. Bring to a boil and add chestnuts. Cook until tender, about 10 to 12 minutes. Drain, reserving liquid and discarding celery and bay leaf. Put chestnuts through a ricer or food processor, and add salt, pepper, and butter. Use a little of the reserved liquid if necessary to correct consistency. Place a dollop of puree onto each Poached Apple Slice.

❖

WILD RICE AND MUSHROOM RING WITH SNAP BEANS

Number of Servings: 10

Preparation Time: 45 minutes

Cooking Time: 2 hours, 10 minutes

INGREDIENTS:

6-ounce package long-grain wild rice
8 ounces (uncooked weight) converted white rice
1 pound fresh mushrooms, sliced
½ cup onion, chopped
4 tablespoons butter
2 cups chicken stock
3 eggs, well beaten
Butter for pan
Snap beans (recipe below)

DIRECTIONS:

Cook both wild rice and white rice separately, according to package directions.

Sauté mushrooms and onions in butter. Add white rice and chicken stock. Bring to a boil, cover, and put in a 350-degree oven for 20 minutes. Fold in cooked wild rice and add the well-beaten eggs.

Mix well and fill a 2½-quart buttered ring mold with rice mixture. Place in a 350 degree oven in bain marie for 25 to 30 minutes. Unmold onto a 12-inch platter. Fill center with snap beans. Bain marie is the French term for a double boiler.

SNAP BEANS

Number of Servings: 8

Preparation Time: 10–15 minutes

Cooking Time: 25–30 minutes

INGREDIENTS:

1½ pounds snap beans, cut in ½-inch pieces
1 onion, chopped
4 tablespoons butter
1 pound mild pork sausage
Salt and white pepper to taste

DIRECTIONS:

Clean snap beans and place in boiling salted water, bring back to a boil and cook for 5 minutes or until al dente. Shock in ice water and drain. Sauté onion in butter until golden brown and add sausage. Brown well, cooking for 15 minutes. Drain grease and add sausage and onion mixture to green beans. Season with salt and pepper. Reheat snap beans by sautéing for 5 minutes over high heat.

Fill wild rice and mushroom ring with beans before serving.

CHARLOTTE RUSSE WITH BRANDIED PEACH HALVES

Number of Servings: 8

Preparation Time: 20 minutes

Chilling Time: 2 hours

INGREDIENTS:

1 package ladyfingers, split

Bavarian Cream Filling
1 cup milk
1-inch piece of vanilla
4 egg yolks
½ cup sugar
1 tablespoon gelatin
2 tablespoons water
1 cup heavy cream
Brandied peaches (recipe below)

DIRECTIONS:

Line charlotte mold with wax paper and line with split ladyfingers as follows: begin at the bottom of the mold by placing a piece of ladyfinger cut in a square in the center. Cover the bottom, starting in the center with ladyfingers cut into triangles. Place them close together so that they radiate out from the center like flower petals. Put split ladyfingers, cut side facing in, upright and close together around the sides of the mold. Fill the mold with the bavarian cream.

Bavarian Cream Filling—Scald the milk with the vanilla. Let it stand for 10 minutes to absorb vanilla flavor. Beat the egg yolks with ½ cup sugar until mixture is smooth and creamy. Pour scalded milk gradually into egg mixture, stirring constantly. Cook the mixture in the top of a double boiler over simmering water, stirring constantly, until thick and smooth. Remove the vanilla by straining the cream into a chilled bowl, and add 1 tablespoon gelatin (softened in 2 tablespoons of cool water and dissolved over hot water). Whisk the mixture, cool it, pour mixture into ladyfinger-lined charlotte mold. Chill for 2 hours. To serve, unmold the charlotte on a round serving dish and garnish with brandied peaches.

❖

BRANDIED PEACHES

Yield: 4 or 5 pint jars

Preparation Time: 20 minutes

Cooking Time: 25 minutes

INGREDIENTS:

5 cups sugar
3 cups water
4 pounds fresh peaches, halved and pitted
Brandy

DIRECTIONS:

Combine the sugar and water in an enameled kettle, and bring the liquid to a boil. Boil for 5 minutes. Add a few peaches at a time and cook them for 5 to 10 minutes, or until they can be easily pierced by a straw. Remove peaches and pack in sterilized jars. Boil remaining liquid until it is thick. Measure the cooled syrup and add 1 pint brandy for every pint of syrup. Combine. Fill jars with syrup and seal at once. Store the jars in a cool place. Let the brandied peaches mellow for at least 2 weeks before using.

GOURMET'S TERRACE DINNER FOR TWO

*C*lassic beauty is often found in simplicity. A dinner for two alfresco—where nature is the sole decorator—can be as elegant and romantic as a meal in the finest restaurant. This is certainly true at Winterthur, where a quiet, intimate evening on the terrace is interrupted only by the gentle babbling of Clenny Run.

This lovely outdoor spot, surrounded by century-old trees, lush shrubbery, and wide expanses of lawn, is ideally suited to be the site of a "Terrace Dinner for Two" from *Gourmet* magazine.

An elegant menu sets this terrace dinner apart from an everyday cookout. Perfectly Grilled Filets Mignons, accompanied by Garlic and Pimento Mayonnaise rather than by a more usual condiment or sauce, take the place of ground beef or steak. Delectable Rosemary Potato Balls replace potato salad or baked potatoes. Steamed Summer Squash is seasoned with garden-fresh basil and freshly ground Parmesan cheese. Kahlúa Coffee Jelly with Cinnamon Cream, served with Wafers of Brown Sugar, is just the right blend of sweet and savory to end this summer meal alfresco.

A single glass hurricane lamp and a crystal vase filled with fat peonies are exquisitely simple accents that add sparkle to this table setting at twilight. The white linen and dinnerware are classically understated, echoing the calm of the descending evening. In contrast are elaborate eighteen-karat-gold goblets, said to have found their way into Winterthur's collection as an expression of remorse from a guest who had broken an antique wineglass at a dinner with Mr. du Pont. These lavish goblets add elegance to an otherwise peaceful table for two.

Gourmet suggests serving this intimate dinner with a Marcarini Barolo la Serra '84. For those who prefer, a rich iced coffee, sweetened but not lightened, makes a grand accompaniment to this summer evening meal.

The Winterthur Gallery terrace, overlooking lovely Clenny Run stream, is the perfect setting for an early dinner served on stately wrought-iron garden furniture. On the table, Chinese porcelain plates and a salt to match, ca. 1800, probably made for a Continental family, complement the eighteen-karat-gold goblets, ca. 1920, made by Bailey, Banks and Biddle of Philadelphia. Other items shown include silverware by Reed & Barton, a glass hurricane lamp, and a glass vase from private collections.

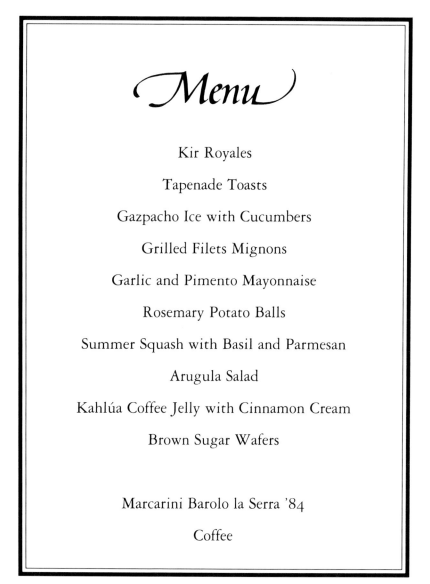

Menu

Kir Royales

Tapenade Toasts

Gazpacho Ice with Cucumbers

Grilled Filets Mignons

Garlic and Pimento Mayonnaise

Rosemary Potato Balls

Summer Squash with Basil and Parmesan

Arugula Salad

Kahlúa Coffee Jelly with Cinnamon Cream

Brown Sugar Wafers

Marcarini Barolo la Serra '84

Coffee

Menu and recipes reprinted with permission from Gourmet.

PREPARATION TIPS: BARBECUE

One of the delights of a terrace dinner is cooking on a grill. From a strictly practical point of view, cooking on a grill keeps kitchens cool and makes hot food more directly accessible to the dinner table. But more important, the smell of charcoal, the glow of embers in the twilight, and the taste of grilled food evoke fond memories of summers past and romantic dreams of summers yet to come.

Barbecued dishes need not be limited to the ubiquitous hamburger or hot dog. A number of foods are delicious when prepared on a grill. Vegetables such as eggplant, summer squash, tomatoes, peppers, and onions take on a very special flavor if they are rubbed with seasoned oil and quickly roasted over hot coals. Corn in its husk or potatoes in their skins can be cooked on the grill or, wrapped in foil, cooked directly on the embers beneath. Many varieties of fish and shellfish, including scallops and shrimp, are delicious grilled on skewers.

When grilling foods, follow a few rules. To prevent sticking, grease or oil the barbecue rack if the foods to be grilled are not naturally fatty (most fish, and all vegetables). Be sure to monitor the heat of the grill. Meat should be cooked very hot initially, to sear in juices; then the heat should be lowered for complete cooking. Vegetables should be cooked very hot and quickly, so that they retain their crispness and flavor.

If grilling over charcoal, pile the coals to light them; then, once they are white at the edges, spread them thinly across the bottom of the grill. Wait until the coals are covered with a fine white powder over a glowing red core before cooking.

For grease flare-ups, keep salt handy to pour over the coals (*never* on the food). Do not use water on flare-ups; it will douse the coals, and water is very dangerous on a gas or electric grill. Never use a charcoal grill indoors unless the grill is in a well-ventilated fireplace with a well-drawing chimney. Charcoal fires produce carbon monoxide that can be fatal in closed spaces.

KIR ROYALES

Yield: 2 drinks

Preparation Time: 5–8 minutes

INGREDIENTS:

4 teaspoons crème de cassis (a liqueur made of black raspberries), plus additional in a shallow dish for dipping the rims of the glasses
Sugar in a shallow dish for dipping the rims of the glasses
1 half-bottle (12.7 ounces) champagne, chilled

DIRECTIONS:

Dip the rims of 2 champagne glasses into the additional crème de cassis, letting the excess drop off. Dip the the glass rims in the sugar. Pour 2 teaspoons of the crème de cassis into each glass and fill the glasses with champagne.

TAPENADE TOASTS

Number of Servings: 6 toasts

Preparation Time: 15–20 minutes

INGREDIENTS:

¼ pound (⅔ cup) Niçoise or Kalamate olives
3 flat anchovy fillets, plus 1 teaspoon of the oil
1 tablespoon capers, drained
1 tablespoon olive oil
6 thin slices French bread, lightly toasted
2 quail eggs or 1 chicken egg, hard-boiled and sliced, for garnish if desired

DIRECTIONS:

Kalamate olives are Greek olives. They can be found at local markets or specialty shops.

With the flat side of a heavy knife crush the olives lightly, discarding the pits. In a food processor, puree the olives with the anchovies, the anchovy oil, the capers, and the olive oil, scraping down the sides often. Spread some of the tapenade on each slice of toast and, if desired, garnish with a slice of egg.

❖

GAZPACHO ICE WITH CUCUMBERS

Number of Servings: 2

Preparation Time: 45–60 minutes

Cooking Time: 5 minutes

Freezing: 2–3 hours, or overnight

INGREDIENTS:

1 teaspoon unflavored gelatin
2 tablespoons dry white wine
½ pound tomatoes, peeled, seeded, and chopped
¼ cup cucumber, peeled, seeded, and finely chopped
¼ cup red bell pepper, finely chopped
2 tablespoons red onion, minced
1 tablespoon olive oil
¾ teaspoon salt
½ teaspoon garlic, minced
⅛ teaspoon cayenne pepper
Paper-thin slices of cucumber, soaked in a bowl of ice and cold water for 15 minutes, drained, and patted dry

DIRECTIONS:

In a small saucepan, let the gelatin soften in the wine for 5 minutes and heat the mixture over low heat, stirring, until the gelatin is dissolved. In a blender, puree the tomatoes with the cucumber, the bell pepper, the onion, the oil, the salt, the garlic, the cayenne, and the gelatin mixture, and freeze the puree in an ice-cream freezer according to the manufacturer's instructions. (Alternatively, freeze the puree in an ice-cube tray for 1 to 2 hours, or until it is frozen, and in a food processor grind the ice until it is smooth but still frozen.) Working quickly, using a small oval ice-cream scoop, scoop the gazpacho ice into 6 ovals, cover with foil, and freeze for at least 1 hour or overnight.

Let the gazpacho ice stand at room temperature for 5 minutes before serving. Reserving 2 cucumber slices for garnish, arrange the remaining cucumber slices decoratively on 2 chilled salad plates, top them with the gazpacho ice, and garnish each serving with a reserved cucumber slice folded decoratively.

❖

GRILLED FILETS MIGNONS

Number of Servings: 2

Preparation Time: 20–25 minutes, plus time to get coals ready

Cooking Time: 8–10 minutes

INGREDIENTS:

2 1-inch-thick filets mignons (6 or 7 ounces each)
2 slices of lean bacon
2 teaspoons black pepper, coarsely ground
Salt
2 fresh rosemary sprigs for garnish, if desired
Garlic and pimiento mayonnaise as an accompaniment

DIRECTIONS:

Pat the filets dry with paper towels, wrap a slice of bacon around the edge of each filet, and secure the bacon with kitchen string. Rub 1 teaspoon of the pepper onto the cut sides of each filet and grill the filets, sprinkled with salt to taste, on an oiled grill over glowing coals for 4 to 5 minutes on each side, or until they are springy to the touch for medium-rare meat. Transfer the filets to a cutting board and discard the string and the bacon. Let the filets stand for 5 minutes and slice them thin. Arrange the slices, overlapping them slightly, on 2 heated plates, and garnish each plate with a rosemary sprig if desired. Serve the filets with the garlic and pimiento mayonnaise.

GARLIC AND PIMIENTO MAYONNAISE

Yield: ½ cup

Preparation Time: 25–30 minutes

The mayonnaise may be made up to 2 days in advance and kept covered and chilled.

INGREDIENTS:

1 garlic clove, minced
½ teaspoon salt, or to taste
1 large egg yolk
1 teaspoon fresh lemon juice, or to taste
½ cup olive oil, extra virgin
Black pepper to taste
2 tablespoons pimiento, drained and minced
⅛ teaspoon cayenne pepper

DIRECTIONS:

In a mortar, with a pestle, mash the garlic with the salt to a paste. Transfer the paste to a small bowl and whisk in the egg yolk and the lemon juice. Add ¼ cup of the oil, drop by drop, whisking constantly, and the remaining oil in a slow stream, whisking constantly. Season the garlic mayonnaise with extra lemon juice, salt, and black pepper to taste. In a food processor or blender, puree the pimento with ¼ cup of the garlic mayonnaise and the cayenne, scraping down the sides often. Spoon the garlic mayonnaise and the pimiento mayonnaise into a small serving dish, and combine.

ROSEMARY POTATO BALLS

Number of Servings: 2

Preparation Time: 20 minutes

Cooking Time: 15–20 minutes

INGREDIENTS:

1 pound boiling potatoes
1 tablespoon unsalted butter
1 tablespoon olive oil
1 teaspoon rosemary leaves, freshly chopped
Salt and pepper to taste

DIRECTIONS:

Peel the potatoes and put them in a bowl of cold water. With a ½-inch melon-ball cutter, cut out balls from the potatoes, reserving the scraps for another use. In a small saucepan of boiling salted water, simmer the potato balls for 5 to 6 minutes, or until they are just tender. Drain well and pat dry. In a skillet, heat the butter and the oil over moderately high heat until the foam subsides; in the fat, sauté the potatoes with the rosemary. Salt and pepper to taste, stirring, for 3 to 5 minutes, or until potatoes are golden.

SUMMER SQUASH WITH BASIL AND PARMESAN

Number of Servings: 2

Preparation Time: 10–15 minutes

Cooking Time: 2–4 minutes

INGREDIENTS:

½ pound summer squash, trimmed and cut crosswise
  into ¼-inch slices
1 tablespoon olive oil
2 tablespoons fresh basil leaves, shredded
Salt and pepper
1 tablespoon Parmesan cheese, freshly grated

DIRECTIONS:

In a steamer set over boiling water, steam the squash, covered, for 2 minutes, or until it is just tender, and transfer it to a bowl. Drizzle the squash with the oil, sprinkle it with the basil, and season it with salt and pepper. Let the squash cool to room temperature. Serve the squash sprinkled with the Parmesan.

ARUGULA SALAD

Number of Servings: 2

Preparation Time: 15–20 minutes

INGREDIENTS:

¼ teaspoon Dijon mustard
1 teaspoon balsamic vinegar or red wine vinegar
Salt and pepper
2 tablespoons olive oil
1 small bunch arugula, stems discarded, washed well
    and spun dry

DIRECTIONS:

In a small bowl, whisk together the mustard and the vinegar, and add salt and pepper to taste; add the oil in a stream, whisking, and whisk the dressing until it is emulsified. Add the arugula, tossing it to coat it with the dressing, and divide the salad between 2 chilled salad plates.

KAHLÚA COFFEE JELLY WITH CINNAMON CREAM

Number of Servings: 2

Preparation Time: 35 minutes, plus 2 hours chilling time

Cooking Time: 5–8 minutes

INGREDIENTS:

Jelly
2 teaspoons unflavored gelatin
2 tablespoons water
¾ cup hot strong coffee
1½ tablespoons sugar
3 tablespoons Kahlúa

Cinnamon Cream
¼ cup heavy cream, well chilled
1 teaspoon honey
⅛ teaspoon cinnamon
2 candied violets, for garnish, if desired

DIRECTIONS:

Jelly—In a small saucepan, let the gelatin soften in 2 tablespoons of water for 5 minutes; heat the mixture over low heat, stirring, until the gelatin is dissolved, and remove the pan from the heat. In a metal bowl, combine the coffee and the sugar, stirring until the sugar is dissolved, and stir in the Kahlúa and the gelatin mixture. Set the bowl in a larger bowl of ice and cold water and stir the mixture occasionally until it is the consistency of raw egg white. Pour ¼ cup of the jelly into each of 2 stemmed glasses and chill it, covered, for 20 minutes.

Beat the remaining coffee jelly with an electric mixer until it is pale and frothy, spoon it into the glasses, and chill, covered, for 2 hours, or until it is set.

Cinnamon Cream—In a chilled bowl, beat the cream with the honey and the cinnamon until it just holds soft peaks. Spoon dollops of the cinnamon cream onto the jelly, and garnish each dessert with a candied violet, if desired. Candied violets are available at specialty food shops.

BROWN SUGAR WAFERS

Yield: about 50 wafers

Preparation Time: 15–18 minutes

Cooking Time: 4–6 minutes

INGREDIENTS:

    2 tablespoons unsalted butter, softened
    ¼ cup light brown sugar, lightly packed
    1 large egg white, beaten lightly
    5 tablespoons all-purpose flour

DIRECTIONS:

In a bowl, using an electric mixer, cream the butter with the brown sugar until the mixture is light and fluffy. Add the egg white a little at a time, beating slowly, and beat the mixture for 5 seconds, or until it is smooth. Sift the flour over the mixture and fold it in thoroughly. Transfer the batter to a pastry bag fitted with a ¼-inch plain tip and pipe 2-inch lengths of it 2 inches apart on lightly greased baking sheets.

Bake the wafers in the middle of a preheated 400-degree oven for 4 to 6 minutes, or until the edges are golden. Let the wafers cool on the baking sheets for 30 seconds, transfer them carefully with a metal spatula to racks, and let them cool completely. If the wafers become too firm to remove from the baking sheets, return them to the oven for about 1 minute to soften.

JOHN LEIGH SPATH'S DINNER FOR TWO: A ROMANTIC CELEBRATION

John Leigh Spath's association with Winterthur began in 1982 when Albert Van Luit & Company became a licensee in the museum's reproductions program. As Director of Design at Van Luit, Mr. Spath has been responsible for some of Winterthur's most beautiful wallpaper and fabric designs. He paints impressionist landscapes that echo the style of the masters of the eighteenth and nineteenth centuries. Mr. Spath has had several West Coast showings, and his oil paintings and wall coverings are featured in some of the finest homes, including the White House, Buckingham Palace, and Prince Charles's town house.

A master's touch is evident in the Spath style of entertaining as well. This romantic early summer dinner bears his trademarks. Classic design elements, minute attention to detail, and—yes—Spath designs on the table and covering the walls add up to a truly memorable dinner à deux.

The table setting is timeless, yet unique. Chinese export porcelain dinnerware from the late eighteenth century is decorated with a vibrant, contemporary-looking aqua glaze. Each place setting is delightfully accented by individual snuffboxes and jars in silver, porcelain, and glass, some dating as early as 1700.

The menu includes dishes noteworthy for both ease of preparation and sumptuous presentation. A distinct delight of this "make-any-occasion-special" meal are the giant strawberries steeped in brandy and coated with rich, dark chocolate.

Candlelight, flowers, delicious food, and leisurely conversation conjure up an image completed by glasses raised in an intimate toast. Spath suggests both wine and champagne to go along with this meal. A California rosé is recommended, light enough for seafood but with enough body to accompany the chicken. The sinfully delicious dessert should be accompanied by a brut champagne and a rich, dark coffee.

Menu

Summer Soup

Shrimp and Salmon Salad

Stuffed Boneless Chicken with Apricot-Brandy Glaze

Cranberry and Cherry Aspic

Belgian Asparagus

Brandied Strawberries Dipped in Chocolate

California Rosé

Champagne

PREPARATION TIPS: GARNISHING

An eye for color, detail, and pattern is essential in John Leigh Spath's work. He carries these qualities into his innovative ideas on food presentation as well. Keep garnishes relatively simple and, always, edible. Be sure to use foods that work well together both visually and in taste.

This menu provides ample opportunity for experimenting with garnishes. Spath suggests several. Top the soup with a dollop of sour cream or plain yogurt and small sprigs of parsley (a cold cucumber soup benefits from yogurt and fresh dill, while a gazpacho is terrific with fresh basil). Serve the shrimp and salmon salad on a bed of tender Bibb or Boston lettuce garnished with freshly cooked halved artichoke hearts.

Tie a ribbon of red pimento around the white Belgian asparagus for a bit of flair, or fan-sliced dried apricots, soaked in warm water to restore the plumpness, in a half moon around the stuffed boneless chicken. Make the pièce de résistance, the chocolate-dipped strawberries, even more irresistible—place two or three of them on a plate with a few delicate sprigs of mint and thinly sliced kiwi. Leave the tops and stems on the strawberries for easier dipping and eating.

Winterthur's "Andover" reproduction wall covering and fabric, taken from a French wood-block printed cotton, ca. 1790, sets the stage for the rich turquoise-glazed Chinese porcelain, ca. 1795. The dishes were probably made for the Continental market. The center medallion bears a coronet, probably that of a viscount. The gilded metal snuffbox, ca. 1700, with a protective covering of isinglass, and the aquamarine enamel-coated jar on copper, ca. 1760, complement the Limoges pear box. The candlestick, ca. 1810, is from a private collection. The silverware is from Reed & Barton.

SUMMER SOUP

Number of Servings: 4

Preparation Time: 25 minutes

Cooking Time: 25–30 minutes

INGREDIENTS:

4 cups chicken stock
2–3 carrots, each cut into 4 pieces
½ medium onion, quartered
¼ pound fresh string beans
½–1 cup corn, fresh or frozen
½–2 cups peas, fresh or frozen
Salt and pepper to taste
½ cup light cream
Sour cream and chopped parsley for garnish

DIRECTIONS:

In large soup pot, bring to a boil the stock, carrots, onion, string beans, corn, and peas. Cook until vegetables are tender and a nice broth develops. Add salt and pepper to taste. Allow soup to cool a bit, then liquefy in food processor or blender. Blend in cream. Heat again; do not boil. Chill. Garnish with sour cream and chopped parsley.

SHRIMP AND SALMON SALAD

Number of Servings: 2–6

Preparation Time: 10–15 minutes

Cooking Time: 25 minutes

INGREDIENTS:

4–5 cups water
3 allspice berries
2 small bay leaves
1 lemon, sliced
2 dozen medium shrimp
2 salmon steaks (about ¾ to 1 pound total weight)
Juice from 1 lemon
4 tablespoons butter, melted
¾–1 cup watercress, chopped and lightly packed
1 tablespoon dill, fresh or dried
Salt and white pepper to taste
⅓ cup ranch dressing
Marinated artichoke hearts and sprigs of watercress

DIRECTIONS:

Bring water, allspice berries, bay leaves, and lemon slices to a boil in a medium-size pan. Lower heat and add shrimp. Cook for 3 to 5 minutes. Do not boil. Drain and set aside to cool. Place salmon steaks in a covered casserole dish, along with lemon juice and melted butter, and bake for 20 minutes in a 350- to 375-degree oven. Allow to cool. Peel shrimp and place them in a medium-size mixing bowl. Toss in watercress. Flake chunks of salmon into the salad with a fork, removing all bones. Add dill and salt and pepper to taste. Toss with ranch dressing. Serve chilled and garnish with artichoke hearts and sprigs of watercress.

STUFFED BONELESS CHICKEN WITH APRICOT BRANDY GLAZE

Number of Servings: 4

Preparation Time: 40–50 minutes, plus 1 hour soaking time

Cooking Time: 30–35 minutes

INGREDIENTS:

4 boneless chicken breasts, slit to make pockets
2 tablespoons salt
Water
Juice of 6 lemons

Wild Rice Stuffing
½ cup celery, chopped
1 cup scallions, chopped (use entire scallion)
1 cup butter
1 cup mushrooms, sliced
1½ cups cooked wild rice
½ cup seedless grapes, halved
½ cup walnuts, chopped
2 tablespoons parsley, chopped
½ teaspoon thyme
Salt and pepper to taste

Glaze
3 tablespoons cognac or brandy
3 tablespoons butter, melted
4½-ounce jar apricot preserves

DIRECTIONS:

Wild Rice Stuffing—Sauté celery and scallions in ½ cup butter until transparent but not brown. Add sliced mushrooms and cook for 2 to 3 minutes longer. In 2-quart saucepan, melt remaining butter. Blend in celery-scallion mixture, cooked rice, grapes, walnuts, parsley, and thyme. Salt and pepper to taste. Use to stuff chicken breasts.

Chicken—fill each pocket with wild rice stuffing. Secure opening with toothpick. Place stuffed chicken in ovenproof baking dish and baste with lemon juice. Bake for 30 to 35 minutes in a 350-degree oven. When meat is tender to the point of knife, chicken is done.

Glaze—Melt butter in small saucepan. Add cognac and apricot preserves. Heat thoroughly. When ready to serve, spoon sauce over stuffed chicken breasts and serve remaining glaze separately.

CRANBERRY AND CHERRY ASPIC

Yield: 1 mold

Preparation Time: 10–15 minutes, plus 2 hours chilling time

Cooking Time: 10 minutes

INGREDIENTS:

1 16-ounce can pitted cherries
1 16-ounce can jellied cranberry sauce
2 cups fresh cranberries
2 cups fresh cherries
1 cup sweet brandy or sherry
1 cup sugar
1 cup fresh lemon juice, with pulp
½ teaspoon water
1 packet powdered gelatin

DIRECTIONS:

Combine canned fruit, fresh fruit, brandy, sugar, and lemon juice in a suitable saucepan. Add about ½ teaspoon of water and heat over a moderate flame until fresh fruit softens. Prepare gelatin according to packet instructions and add to fruit conserve. Cool mixture and pour it into a wet mold. Chill thoroughly and serve on a chilled platter.

BELGIAN ASPARAGUS

Number of Servings: 2–6

Preparation Time: 5–10 minutes

Cooking Time: 15–20 minutes

INGREDIENTS:

White asparagus (1 to 3 pounds)
4–8 tablespoons butter, melted
Lemon wedges for garnish, along with pimento slices
    for tying the bundles in a "ribbon"

DIRECTIONS:

Steam or boil asparagus until tender. An ideal cooking arrangement allows the stalks to cook in boiling water while the tips cook in steam.

Serve with melted butter, lemon wedges, and pimento bows.

BRANDIED STRAWBERRIES
DIPPED IN CHOCOLATE

Yield: 24 strawberries

Preparation Time: 30 minutes, plus overnight soaking of strawberries

Cooking Time: 10–15 minutes

INGREDIENTS:

1 cup brandy
½ cup sugar, dissolved in ½ cup hot water
24 strawberries, large and in perfect condition
16 ounces dark bittersweet chocolate for dipping
Kiwi, thinly sliced, and fresh mint leaves for garnish

DIRECTIONS:

Combine brandy and sugar mixture in a large container with cover. Add strawberries and soak overnight. Drain strawberries well. In a double boiler (or in a microwave) melt chocolate. Dip strawberries, one by one, into the melted chocolate, making sure not to cover the leaves at the top. (Leave tops and stems on the strawberries for easier dipping and eating.) Put the dipped strawberries on wax paper and chill. Serve with sliced kiwi and mint leaves.

DINNER FOR ONE OR MORE WITH
ART BUCHWALD

*E*ven if the menu were to include nothing more than a peanut butter sandwich, dinner with America's "most huggable man" would surely be a treat. Even so, Art Buchwald offers an enticement here that few mortals could resist. The "Buchwald Baked Potato à la Caviar," stuffed with sour cream and caviar, is, in its creator's estimation, the perfect dinner for a busy world.

Art Buchwald is a well-known humorist, columnist, and author. His syndicated column, by which he has singlehandedly held America's government intact for years, reflects everyday life in this country. Everything, and nothing, about American life is sacred to Mr. Buchwald; his targets range from the occupants of the White House to working wives and house husbands.

Mr. Buchwald's dinner menu is as humorous, irreverent, and practical as he is. To describe the dinner in his words: "This dish is especially good when you're tired and don't want to prepare a full meal. You can eat it every day and never get tired of it. It has a lot of protein and vitamins in it, and doctors recommend it." What more can one ask from a meal?

A dinner this perfect requires a perfectly simple setting. An unadorned plate and exquisite linens and flatware meet all requirements. The only other necessities are ice-cold vodka, preferably a good Russian or Scandinavian variety, and a comfortable chair.

Menu

The Buchwald Baked Potato à la Caviar

Vodka

PREPARATION TIP: "BUCHWALD BAKED POTATO À LA CAVIAR"

The first thing I do is go out and buy the best caviar I can afford. Don't stint! Because you never know when you'll eat caviar again.

Take the caviar home and put it in the ice box; then place one large baked potato in the oven. If you plan to share the caviar with someone else, allow one baked potato for each person.

After the potato is baked, take it out of the oven and slice one quarter off the top, then scoop out the white part of the potato, leaving the skin intact.

Whip the white part up with a little milk until it gets nice and creamy, then put it back into the skin.

Make a little hole in the center, then take the caviar out of the ice box, open it carefully, and put as much as you want into the hole.

Then take a dab of sour cream and put it on top of the caviar and sprinkle a few chives on the sour cream.

Pour a shot of vodka and proceed to eat.

—Art Buchwald

A French porcelain plate, ca. 1850, is the focus for this filling meal. Imported and possibly decorated by Richard Biggs of Boston, the plate is the only example of European porcelain bearing an importer's mark within the Winterthur collection. Other antiques shown include a silver knife, ca. 1810, made by John W. Forbes of New York, and a silver fork, ca. 1815, of Chinese origin. The gilded Dutch tumbler, ca. 1810, is from a private collection, and the brass frog clip comes from Winterthur's Plant Shop.

The Buchwald
Baked Potato a la Caviar

THE BUCHWALD BAKED POTATO
À LA CAVIAR

Number of Servings: 1

Preparation Time: 10 minutes

Cooking Time: 40 minutes

INGREDIENTS:

1 baking potato
1 tablespoon milk
Caviar
3 tablespoons sour cream
1 teaspoon fresh chives

DIRECTIONS:

Place baking potato in a 400-degree oven and bake for 40 minutes. (If using microwave oven, follow manufacturer's cooking instructions.) After the potato is baked, slice ¼ off the top and scoop out the white part, leaving the skin intact. Whip the white part up with a little milk, until it is creamy, and then put it back into the skin. Garnish with plenty of caviar and sour cream. Sprinkle chives on top.

GOLDEN DOOR SPA'S LOW-CALORIE DINNER

The Golden Door, founded in 1959 by Deborah Szekely, is one of the most elegant spas in America. Steeped in tradition, the Golden Door has taught a generation of American men and women the value of good health and a well-balanced diet, anticipating the trend toward healthy eating and exercise. Ms. Szekely has taken these goals further. She is an avid supporter of the Inter-American Foundation, a nonprofit organization dedicated to teaching good nutrition practices at the grassroots level in Mexico, the Caribbean, and Central America.

Under Ms. Szekely's direction, elegance was (as it remains) a key word at the Golden Door, as the remarkable "diet" meals served to guests demonstrate. Ms. Szekely emphasized presentation, with colorful and attractive place settings an essential element. Here, dramatic lusterware is placed on a silver lamé cloth, accented by

Silver and glass objects gleam in the candlelight reflected by a shimmering silver lamé tablecloth.
Antiques shown include copper luster dinnerware, Staffordshire, England, ca. 1810, and glass candlesticks, United States, ca. 1830. Other pieces shown: Winterthur reproductions of Myer Myers beakers, New York, ca. 1760; flatware by Reed & Barton.

the yellow of the candles and dinnerware. Silver beakers and contemporary glass containers for bread sticks and calla lilies encased in glass add even more sparkle to the table top.

Fresh, expertly prepared, and interesting food is a priority as well. Creamy broccoli soup, rich buttered acorn squash, delicately seasoned chicken, and banana ice cream hardly seem like a low-calorie meal.

Along with this meal serve sparkling water with a twist of lemon or lime or a light wine spritzer with a twist.

Menu

Broccoli Soup with Sesame Seeds

Apple-Mushroom Salad

Golden Door Breast of Chicken

Acorn Squash

Garlic Bread Sticks

Banana Ice Cream

Sparkling Water

Sauterne Spritzer

PREPARATION TIP: "LIGHTENED FOOD"

Dieting to lose weight does not preclude eating favorite foods. Almost any food can be "lightened," without giving up taste, texture, or interest, by using lower-calorie alternatives for ingredients with high fat and cholesterol contents.

This wonderful spa menu provides some prime examples of tasty ways to cut calories. Broccoli soup uses low-fat Neufchâtel cheese rather than milk or cream to provide its rich, creamy base. Neufchâtel melts beautifully and is terrific used in soups and sauces as well as in "mock" cheesecake or cheese spreads. A sprinkling of toasted sesame seeds, rather than croutons, is added to the soup for crunch and flavor.

Removing the skin and extra fat on the chicken is an obvious way to save calories. Another, less obvious way is to brown the chicken in just a touch of oil, then transfer the meat to the oven for cooking. Juices are seared in, so the meat remains tender rather than drying out as it often does when it is baked without its skin. Oven cooking saves on calories because extra oil is not used.

An alternative to high-fat, high-calorie desserts is banana ice cream or ice cream made with papaya, peaches, pears, or other dense fruits. Made with low-fat milk and no sugar, this tasty dessert has only about one-fourth the calories in traditional ice cream. Best, though, is the ease of preparation—no ice cream machines are needed here! The only equipment required is a blender or food processor and a freezer. And the dish can be prepared just two hours before dinner.

Other ways of lightening food include using plain yogurt instead of sour cream; poaching or baking fish or meat in its own broth rather than frying or baking it in a heavy sauce; steaming vegetables rather than sautéing them; and serving vegetables, including potatoes, without butter or heavy sauces. Keep food interesting by experimenting with herbs and spices to replace gravies and high-calorie condiments.

BROCCOLI SOUP WITH SESAME SEEDS

Number of Servings: 4

Preparation Time: 20 minutes

Cooking Time: 55 minutes

144 calories per serving

INGREDIENTS:

2 teaspoons sesame or safflower oil
1 teaspoon garlic, minced
1 onion, diced
2 cups broccoli stems and tops cut in 1-inch pieces
2 teaspoons dried sweet basil
1 teaspoon vegetable seasoning (such as Spike or Vegit)
4 cups vegetable stock, heated
2 ounces Neufchâtel low-fat cream cheese
½ cup broccoli flowerets
2 tablespoons raw sesame seeds, freshly toasted

DIRECTIONS:

In heavy saucepan, heat oil. Gently sauté garlic and onion until glazed. Add basil and broccoli stems and tops. Sprinkle with vegetable seasoning. Cover saucepan and steam over medium-low heat for 8 to 10 minutes. Add vegetable stock. Simmer gently, uncovered, for 45 minutes, till vegetables are tender. Remove from heat. In blender, combine soup mixture with cheese until smooth.

Reheat mixture to a boil. Quickly steam broccoli flowerets. They should still be crisp when added to the soup. Sprinkle sesame seeds over each bowl before serving.

VEGETABLE STOCK

Number of Servings: 8

Preparation Time: 2 hours, 30 minutes

Cooking Time: 2 hours

11 calories per serving

INGREDIENTS:

whole celery or 1 small celery root
1 onion, peeled, studded with 4 cloves
2 leeks (white part only)
1 carrot
4 ripe tomatoes, quartered
1 turnip, small
1 teaspoon dried whole thyme
2 bay leaves
10 peppercorns, crushed

12 cups water
2 tablespoons soy sauce (low sodium)
1 tablespoon sea salt

DIRECTIONS:

Combine all ingredients in large stockpot. Slowly bring to boil. Simmer about 2 hours, reducing to about 10 cups. Strain liquid. Check seasoning.

✣

APPLE-MUSHROOM SALAD

Number of Servings: 4

Preparation Time: 10 minutes

52 calories per serving

INGREDIENTS:

1 apple, small; washed, cored, and sliced with skin
½ pound fresh mushrooms, sliced
2 tablespoons fresh lemon juice
2 teaspoons sesame or safflower oil
2 tablespoons fresh parsley, chopped
¼ teaspoon vegetable seasoning (such as Spike or Vegit)
Watercress or alfalfa sprouts to line 4 plates

DIRECTIONS:

Combine apple, mushrooms, lemon juice, oil, parsley, and vegetable seasoning. Spoon onto 4 beds of watercress or alfalfa sprouts, and serve.

✣

GOLDEN DOOR BREAST OF CHICKEN

Number of Servings: 4

Preparation Time: 20 minutes

Cooking Time: 30 minutes

266 calories per serving

INGREDIENTS:

2 ounces Monterey Jack cheese, cut into 4 pieces
4 chicken breast halves, skinned, trimmed of fat
2 tablespoons unbleached flour
2 eggs, beaten
1 tablespoon Parmesan or Romano cheese, freshly grated
1 tablespoon chives, chopped
1 tablespoon dried sweet basil, chopped
1 teaspoon vegetable seasoning (such as Spike or Vegit)
2 teaspoons sesame or safflower oil
4 parsley sprigs
4 lemon wedges

DIRECTIONS:

Insert piece of Monterey Jack into pouch of each chicken breast (to make a pouch, push finger along bone). Coat breast with flour, and dip into eggs beaten with Parmesan or Romano cheese, chives, sweet basil, and vegetable seasoning. Preheat oven to 375 degrees.

In heavy skillet, heat oil. Add chicken breasts and brown on both sides. Remove from skillet; place in baking dish. Bake, uncovered, about 25 to 30 minutes, till chicken is tender.

Garnish with parsley and lemon and serve.

✤

ACORN SQUASH

Number of Servings: 4

Preparation Time: 15 minutes

Cooking Time: 45–60 minutes

135 calories per serving

INGREDIENTS:

2 acorn squash, medium size
1 tablespoon butter, melted
2 teaspoons brown sugar
1 teaspoon ground cinnamon
¼ teaspoon grated nutmeg
Dash allspice

DIRECTIONS:

Preheat oven to 350 degrees. Cut squash in half, and scoop out seeds. In separate dish, combine melted butter, sugar, and spices. Divide mixture equally into center of each squash half. Place halves in baking dish filled with water to a depth of 2 inches. Cover with foil and bake 45 to 60 minutes, until tender.

✤

SAUTERNE SPRITZER

Number of Servings: 4

Preparation Time: 5 minutes

113 calories per serving

INGREDIENTS:

1 cup Sauterne wine
1 cup cranberry juice, sugar-free
1 cup soda water
3 tablespoons frozen orange-juice concentrate, thawed
crushed ice
4 orange slices

DIRECTIONS:

Combine all ingredients. Pour over ice in 4 tall glasses. Garnish with orange and serve.

BANANA ICE CREAM

Number of Servings: 4

Preparation Time: 15 minutes, plus 4 hours freezing time

95 calories per serving

INGREDIENTS:

4 bananas, small and ripe
Fresh lemon juice
1 teaspoon vanilla extract
½ cup low-fat milk
12 strawberries (optional)
Mint

DIRECTIONS:

Peel bananas, cut out tips and brown spots, remove strings.

Squeeze lemon juice over bananas. Wrap in plastic bag and freeze until solid.

Chill 4 champagne glasses or bowls. Near serving time, cut bananas into small pieces. Blend in food processor with vanilla extract and milk till very smooth. If mixture becomes too thick, add more milk. Pour into chilled glasses or bowls. Return to freezer for no longer than 2 hours. Garnish each dish with a sprig of mint and serve. *Note*: To give ice cream a pink color, 12 large strawberries may be added when blending.

CHEF TELL'S QUICK CUISINE DINNER

When an occasion calls for a lavish dinner and time is a problem, Chef Tell's "Quick Cuisine" is the answer. Sometimes referred to as a "short-order gourmet," Chef Tell, in his "90-Second Cooking" spot on "Evening Magazine," has brought tasty, elegant dishes into kitchens and dining rooms across the country.

Tell Erhardt is certainly qualified to be a connoisseur of fine dining. A four-time recipient of the coveted Cordon Bleu Award, he was the youngest person in West

Some of the most beautifully colored examples of Chinese export porcelain were sent to Portugal. The plate shown has the coat of arms of Don Antonio José de Castro, Bishop of Oporto between 1789 and 1814. The wineglass, ca. 1765, is blown-waisted with double-spiral opaque white twist elements.
Other items shown include silverware courtesy of the Enchanted Owl and an antique purse from the collection of Carolyn Ferguson.

Germany ever to receive the title "Master Chef," an honor he earned at age twenty-four. An established author and television personality, Chef Tell owns Chef Tell's, a restaurant outside Philadelphia, and Chef Tell Erhardt's Old House in the Cayman Islands.

Several delicious dishes, all of which can be prepared in thirty-five minutes or less, are offered in this Quick Cuisine menu, leaving diners with plenty of time to enjoy a perfect dinner in a perfect setting before they dash off for an exciting evening's entertainment. Colorful Danish Salad, rich almond-coated Chicken Pompadour with Hollandaise Sauce, and Stir-Fried Vegetables can each be prepared in as much time as it takes to broil a hamburger! Cream of Cauliflower Soup can be made in advance and reheated just before serving. White Chocolate Mousse should be prepared well in advance and served thoroughly chilled.

Serve this chicken menu with a light white wine like a fumé blanc or—for a change of pace—a dry blush wine like a cabernet blanc.

Menu

Danish Salad

Cream of Cauliflower Soup

Chicken Pompadour with Sauce Hollandaise

Rice Pilaf

Stir-Fried Vegetables

White Chocolate Mousse with Raspberry Sauce

Fumé Blanc

PREPARATION TIPS: STOCK

One way to speed up the cooking process is to have certain essentials available. Soup stocks particularly lend themselves to freezing and can be made well ahead in bulk and stored for future use.

Good stock takes time to prepare. It is achieved by simmering meat or fish and/or vegetables for several hours and then straining the broth and discarding the solids.

Chef Tell gives several hints for making and storing stocks in his book *Quick Cuisine* (1984). Stock can be frozen in covered containers or stored in jars in the refrigerator. Frozen stock will keep much longer than refrigerated broth. If storing stock in the refrigerator, do not remove the fat layer on the top of the stock; it will act as a preservative, protecting the stock for about a week. Chef Tell recommends discarding stock that has begun to break down and cannot be restored by reboiling.

Stock can be degreased easily by chilling it and removing the solid fat layer from the top. If stock must be degreased while it is warm, Chef Tell recommends running a teaspoon in small circles on the top of the broth, scooping up small spoonfuls of fat. Although this process is time consuming, it is possible to remove most of the fat using this method. Any additional fat can be removed by running a paper towel on top of the stock.

To achieve concentrated stock with a stronger flavor, bring strained stock to a boil and cook it until it has reduced by half. Cool and store the liquid for future use.

DANISH SALAD

Number of Servings: 4

Preparation Time: 25 minutes

INGREDIENTS:

Cucumber Salad
1 cucumber, thinly sliced
Salt and pepper to taste
2 teaspoons oil
2 teaspoons vinegar
1 tablespoon dill, chopped

Radish Salad
1 bunch radishes, thinly sliced
Salt and pepper to taste
1 teaspoon oil
1 teaspoon vinegar

Tomato Salad
1 large or 2 small tomatoes, thinly sliced
Salt and pepper to taste
1 teaspoon oil
1 teaspoon vinegar
1 tablespoon onion, chopped

Endive Salad
1 endive
Bibb or Boston lettuce

2 hard-boiled eggs

DIRECTIONS:

Cucumber Salad—Layer cucumber slices in a dish and sprinkle with salt. Let sit for about 30 minutes. Drain well. Mix together pepper, oil, vinegar, and dill and toss lightly with sliced cucumber.

Radish Salad—Mix together salt, pepper, oil, and vinegar. Toss lightly with radishes.

Tomato Salad—Sprinkle tomato slices with salt, pepper, oil, vinegar, and onion.

Endive Salad—Slice the endive in half lengthwise. Remove the core. Soak in lukewarm water for about 30 minutes. Drain well. Separate leaves. Use a few leaves for each plate.

Assembly—Line 4 salad plates with Bibb or Boston lettuce. Arrange equal portions of the salads on each plate. Garnish each plate with egg slices and a sprig of parsley.

© Tell Erhardt 1987

CREAM OF CAULIFLOWER SOUP

Number of Servings: 4

Preparation Time: 35 minutes

Cooking Time: 50 minutes

INGREDIENTS:

3 quarts water
Juice of 1 lemon
1 head cauliflower
½ cup butter or margarine
½ cup all-purpose flour
½ cup onion, minced
Salt and freshly ground black pepper to taste
½ cup heavy cream
2 egg yolks

DIRECTIONS:

Heat water in a large pot and add lemon juice. Add the whole head of cauliflower and cook for about 10 minutes, or until just barely tender.

Remove the cauliflower, reserving the liquid. Cut off the green leaves and shred them. Break cauliflower into flowerets and set them aside.

Melt the butter and add flour all at once, stirring to make a smooth, creamy mixture. Add shredded cauliflower leaves and the onion and cook for 3 to 4 minutes, stirring occasionally. Let mixture cool. When cool, slowly add the cauliflower poaching liquid. Bring to a simmer and cook for 30 minutes. Season with salt and pepper. Strain the soup through a sieve into another pot. Keep it warm over very low heat.

Beat cream and egg yolks together and add to the hot soup, stirring until thickened. Serve soup garnished with the cauliflower flowerets.

© Tell Erhardt 1987

CHICKEN POMPADOUR WITH SAUCE HOLLANDAISE

Number of Servings: 4–6

Preparation Time: 15–20 minutes

Cooking Time: 20–25 minutes

INGREDIENTS:

6 pieces boneless chicken breast, skinned
Salt and freshly ground black pepper to taste
2 eggs
Flour for dredging

2 cups blanched almonds, chopped
6 tablespoons butter or margarine
Sauce Hollandaise

DIRECTIONS:

Pound chicken breasts lightly to even them. Season them with salt and pepper. Beat the eggs in a flat soup plate. Put a good amount of flour on a piece of wax paper. Place the almonds on another piece of wax paper.

Dredge each chicken breast in the flour, dip it into the eggs, and then coat it with the almonds. Press with the palm of your hand so that the almonds stick to the chicken. Melt butter in a large frying pan and sauté the chicken breasts for 4 to 5 minutes on each side, or until golden brown. Reduce heat and continue cooking for about 15 to 20 minutes or until chicken is done. Serve immediately with Sauce Hollandaise.

© Tell Erhardt 1987

SAUCE HOLLANDAISE

Yield: 1 cup
Preparation Time: 20—25 minutes
Cooking Time: 5—10 minutes

INGREDIENTS:

6 egg yolks
½ cup dry white wine
1 pound unsalted butter for 12 ounces clarified butter
Salt and freshly ground black pepper to taste

DIRECTIONS:

Put the egg yolks and wine into heavy saucepan. Beat together over medium heat until mixture is thickened. Remove from heat and continue to beat until the mixture cools a little.

Beat in the clarified butter with a wire whisk, beating until the ingredients are well combined. Season with salt and pepper. Do not reheat the sauce; if it must be kept warm, place it over a pot of hot water.

Note: If you are hesitant about putting the saucepan directly over the heat, you can combine the egg yolks and wine in the top of a double boiler over gently boiling water. Remember, too, that the egg yolk mixture and the clarified butter should be at about the same temperature (140 degrees) to combine properly.

Clarified Butter—Put 1 pound of butter in a small saucepan and melt it over high heat. As it bubbles, a foam will come to the surface. When this foam subsides and sinks to the bottom of the pan, pour off the clear portion of butter at the top—this is the clarified butter.

© Tell Erhardt 1987

RICE PILAF

Number of Servings: 4

Preparation Time: 10 minutes

Cooking Time: 20–25 minutes

INGREDIENTS:

2–3 tablespoons butter or margarine
1 small onion, finely chopped
1 cup rice
2 cups chicken stock

DIRECTIONS:

Melt butter in an ovenproof casserole or saucepan. Add the onion and sauté until it turns translucent. Add the rice; cook and stir for a few minutes to coat all of the grains of rice with butter. Add the stock and bring to a boil. Cover and bake in a 375-degree oven for about 18 minutes or, if you prefer, cook over low heat on the stove.

© Tell Erhardt 1987

STIR-FRIED VEGETABLES

Number of Servings: 4

Preparation Time: 15–25 minutes

Cooking Time: 9–10 minutes

INGREDIENTS:

4 tablespoons butter or margarine
1 cup onion, diced
2 cups broccoli flowerets
2 cups cauliflower flowerets
2 yellow squash, trimmed and sliced
8 mushrooms, cut in half
Salt to taste
4 tablespoons water

DIRECTIONS:

Melt butter in a frying pan and add the onion. Sauté for 4 to 5 minutes. Add the broccoli, cauliflower, squash, and mushrooms. Season with salt and add the water. Cover the pan and cook for about 5 minutes, or until the vegetables are just crisp. Serve hot.

© Tell Erhardt 1987

WHITE CHOCOLATE MOUSSE
WITH RASPBERRY SAUCE

Number of Servings: 6–8

Preparation Time: 15–20 minutes

Cooking Time: 3–6 minutes

INGREDIENTS:

> 1 cup heavy cream
> ½ cup sugar
> ½ cup water
> 3 egg whites
> ½ pound white chocolate, finely chopped

DIRECTIONS:

Whip the heavy cream and refrigerate until ready to use. In saucepan, bring the sugar and water to a boil and cook for a few minutes, to form a syrup. Place the egg whites in a mixing bowl, beating until they are fairly stiff. With the motor on, pour the hot syrup slowly into the egg whites. Continue to beat at high speed for a few more minutes. Fold the chopped chocolate into the egg whites, then fold in the whipped cream.

Pour into individual serving dishes or wine goblets and chill.

© Tell Erhardt 1987

❖

RASPBERRY SAUCE

Number of Servings: 6–8

Preparation Time: 10 minutes

INGREDIENTS:

> 1 package frozen raspberries, thawed, or 1 pint fresh
>   raspberries, rinsed
> 2 tablespoons sugar
> 1 ounce Kirschwasser (German cherry brandy)

DIRECTIONS:

Put the raspberries, sugar, and kirsch in the container of a blender or food processor and puree. Strain the sauce and pour it over or around each serving of white chocolate mousse.

© Tell Erhardt 1987

COUNTRY DINNER BY
MR. AND MRS. LEO RABKIN

A country dinner with Mr. and Mrs. Leo Rabkin means a chance to view their extraordinary collection of American folk art and antique toys. Like Henry Francis du Pont, who began his collection with hooked rugs, Windsor chairs, and spatterware (spatter-decorated glazed earthenware), the Rabkins recognized early the importance of folk art and of America's rural traditions. An abstract painter, Mr. Rabkin finds inspiration in the animation of folk-art objects, the way they imitate the human form. Having built the definitive whirligig collection before it was fashionable, the Rabkins have turned to more contemporary carved-stone folk art, and early paintings by black artists.

An autumn dinner with the Rabkins draws on Mrs. Rabkin's German roots for its special charm and flavor. Cold Beet Soup, with a dollop of sour cream, starts the meal; Oven-Fried Fish and spicy Ratatouille provide its body. Applesauce, fruit-filled tarts, and golden cheesecake round out a dinner that has the "taste of the old country."

Folk art sets the tone for the dinner table, with colorfully glazed Pennsylvania German plates highlighting each place. Heavy colored glass goblets carry on the country mood. Whimsical table decorations include an earthenware "squirrel pitcher" and other stylized figurines. Agate-handled steel cutlery and pewter pitchers and flasks add substance to the setting.

Serve this meal with a good dark German or English beer. For those who prefer wine, try a fairly dry German white, like a Kabinett. Apple cider served in pewter mugs also makes an appropriate thirst quencher.

The Fraktur Room at Winterthur, with its painted woodwork from the David Hottenstein House, ca. 1783, of Kutztown, Pennsylvania, is warmed by the country table set with "tortoise shell" earthenware plates, ca. 1765.

Other antiques shown include round-ended pistol-handled flatware, ca. 1750, from England; an earthenware pug dog, ca. 1760, from Staffordshire, England; an English agate-ware cat, ca. 1740; an English agate-ware rooster, ca. 1740; an earthenware squirrel used as a bottle, ca. 1806, from Strasburg, Virginia; a pewter flagon, ca. 1766, and a pewter flask, ca. 1754, made by Johann Christophe of Lancaster, Pennsylvania; and green lead wineglasses, ca. 1800, from England. The Fraktur Room is named after the collection of Pennsylvania German illuminated documents that adorn its walls—baptismal certificates, wedding documents, and so on, all executed in ornate "Fraktur"-style calligraphy.

Menu

Cold Beet Soup

Oven-Fried Fish

Ratatouille

Applesauce

Pear Tart

Golden Cheesecake

White Wine or Dark Beer

Coffee

PREPARATION TIPS: TART SHELLS

Tart shells can be filled with almost anything, sweet or savory. For sweet tarts, filled with custard, fresh or stewed fruits, mousse, or Bavarian cream, use the recipe that follows. For savory tarts, with steamed seafood, meat, or vegetable fillings, omit most of the sugar from the recipe, leaving approximately two tablespoons, and add salt to taste.

When forming the shell in the tart pan, press rather than roll the dough. It will shrink less when baked if stretching is kept to a minimum. Prick holes at regular intervals to let steam escape and to keep the dough from buckling.

Prepare the tart fillings separately and fill the shells just before serving. The shells are very flaky and fragile, more so than traditional piecrust, and will absorb liquid rapidly. Shells will deteriorate when they become wet.

COLD BEET SOUP

Number of Servings: 8

Preparation Time: 20 minutes

Cooking Time: 25 minutes

INGREDIENTS:

2 cups fresh grated beets (about 8 medium-sized beets)
½ cup potatoes, peeled and diced
½ cup scallions, chopped (reserve 2 tablespoons)
¼ cup carrots, shredded
½ teaspoon sour salt (citric acid)
1 teaspoon sugar
6 cups water
6 cups chicken broth (2 24-ounce cans)
3 eggs
Sour cream

DIRECTIONS:

Combine beets, potatoes, scallions, carrots, salt, sugar, water and chicken broth in a large kettle. Bring to a boil and let simmer for 25 minutes. Beat eggs lightly in a large bowl with an electric mixer. Pour boiling hot soup liquid in a steady stream into bowl with mixer running all the time. Continue mixing for 2 minutes to keep eggs from curdling. After soup has cooled, pour into a covered jar and let sit in the refrigerator for at least 6 hours. Best overnight.

Pour cold beet soup into serving bowls, add dollop of sour cream, and garnish with remaining scallions.

✤

OVEN FRIED FISH

Number of Servings: 8

Preparation Time: 15 minutes

Cooking Time: 20 minutes

INGREDIENTS:

1 cup butter
8 small whole fish or fillets
2 egg yolks
⅔ cup light cream
2 cups fine bread crumbs
Salt and pepper
Lemon wedges

DIRECTIONS:

If using whole fish, have your fish cleaned and filleted at the market. Melt butter and pour half of it over the bottom of a baking dish lined with foil. Preheat the oven to 500 degrees and heat the baking dish for 4 minutes before placing the fish in it.

Beat egg yolks with cream, and salt and pepper to taste. Dip each fillet in egg mixture and roll it in the bread crumbs. When all the fish are coated and the baking dish is hot, arrange the fish in the dish and pour the rest of the melted butter over them.

Bake for 15 minutes or until the fish flakes easily when tested with a fork.

Serve with a lemon wedge.

✤

RATATOUILLE

Number of Servings: 8–10

Preparation Time: 40–45 minutes, plus 1 hour for eggplant standing time

Cooking Time: 30–40 minutes baking time, 20–25 minutes frying time

INGREDIENTS:

Pure olive oil, about 1 tablespoon for each vegetable
5 medium onions, ring sliced
2 cloves of garlic, pressed
2 pounds zucchini squash, sliced thinly
6 small eggplants, peeled and cut in small cubes, sprinkled with salt and placed in a plastic-wrap-covered bowl with a heavy weight on top to squeeze out all the juice; this can take an hour.
1 pound green peppers, cut in small slices
3 pounds plum tomatoes, peeled and sliced (Place tomatoes in boiling water, a few at a time, for just a few moments. Remove with a fork and peel when cooled.)
Salt and Pepper

DIRECTIONS:

Put a tablespoon or so of olive oil in a large frying pan and begin to fry the sliced onions, stirring constantly. Onions should be transparent when done, not browned. Remove from heat and place onions in a layer in a large casserole dish. Using the same frying pan for all the vegetables, add the garlic, more olive oil, and the sliced zucchini. Cook only till partly done, stirring constantly. Transfer to casserole and layer on top of the onions.

Fry the prepared eggplant in more olive oil. Do so quickly; eggplant tends to stick to the pan. Arrange in a layer on top of the zucchini. Fry the green pepper slices and place them on top of the eggplant. To finish, place the sliced tomatoes, which have cooled, on top of the casserole. Sprinkle with pepper and a little salt. A few tablespoons of olive oil can be added now. Cover casserole with aluminum foil or matching lid and bake for 30 to 40 minutes in a 350-degree oven.

✥

APPLESAUCE

Number of Servings: 8

Preparation Time: 10 minutes

Cooking Time: 15–25 minutes

INGREDIENTS:

6 pounds greenings (tart apples)
2 cups apple juice or water

1 cup sugar
½ teaspoon cinnamon

DIRECTIONS:

Cut each apple in quarters, removing the flower (little black strands) from the bottom and the stem. Leave peel, core, and especially the seeds in. Place the apples in a large pot and pour the liquid over them as quickly as possible, before the apples start to turn brown. Bring to a boil, turn down the heat, and continue to simmer until the apples are completely soft and mushy. This will take from 10 to 20 minutes. Put the apples through a food mill or strainer into a bowl already containing the sugar and cinnamon. Mix thoroughly and sweeten to taste.

PEAR TART

Yield: 10-inch tart

Preparation Time: 20 minutes

Cooking Time: 20 minutes

INGREDIENTS:

Shell
¼ cup sugar
1¼ cups flour
1 hard-boiled egg yolk
1 raw egg yolk
1 stick butter

Filling
8 large pears
1 cup sugar
2 tablespoons arrowroot
1 cup water

DIRECTIONS:

Shell—Mix sugar, flour, and hard-boiled egg yolk thoroughly. (Using your hands, rub egg yolk into the sugar and flour mixture.) Add the raw egg yolk and keep mixing until the mixture looks light yellow and there are no lumps. Melt the butter, cool off slightly, and put into the flour mixture. Mix well with your hands. The dough will form into a ball. Press dough into a 10-inch buttered tart pan. Using a fork, prick around the edge and all over the bottom. This is very important, as the dough will buckle otherwise. Bake in a 375-degree preheated oven for 12 minutes. Check constantly as soon as the edges start to get slightly brown. Take tart out of the oven because, with its rather high fat content, it continues baking. Cool.

Filling—Peel and quarter pears. Remove cores and cut into thin slices. Use 1 cup of the sliced pears, 1 cup sugar, and ¾ cup water and cook over low flame for 5 minutes. Mix ¼ cup water with arrowroot and incorporate it into the fruit mixture. Let the mixture come to a boil and cook, stirring constantly, until it becomes thick. Cool slightly, and pour half of the mixture into the tart shell. Arrange sliced pears in the tart shell and pour the remaining glaze over the top. Chill.

Note: This dough, mixed with ground almonds and shaped into little crescents, makes a wonderful cookie.

GOLDEN CHEESECAKE

Yield: 1 8-inch cheesecake

Preparation Time: 40 minutes

Cooking Time: 50–70 minutes

INGREDIENTS:

Bottom Crust
4 ounces butter
2 ounces cream cheese
3 tablespoons sugar
1 egg
2 tablespoons baking powder
Dash of salt
1⅓ cups flour

Cheese Filling
3 tablespoons golden raisins
1 tablespoon brandy, cognac, or other liqueur
1 cup cream cheese
1 cup cottage cheese
¼ cup sugar
1 tablespoon flour
3 eggs, separated
1 teaspoon melted butter

1 teaspoon grated lemon rind
½ teaspoon vanilla

DIRECTIONS:

Bottom Crust—Cream butter, cream cheese, sugar, and egg together. Add baking powder and salt to flour and sift into cheese mixture. Using an 8-inch or 9-inch springform pan, press the dough onto the bottom and halfway up the sides. Prick dough all over with a fork and prebake in a 350-degree oven for 5 to 10 minutes. Watch that crust does not get brown. Remove from oven and let cool.

Cheese Filling—Mix raisins with brandy and set aside to soak. Cream together cheeses, sugar, and flour. Stir in egg yolks, then melted butter, lemon rind, and vanilla. Add soaked raisins. Stiffly beat the egg whites and fold them into the cheese mixture. Pour into the cooled bottom crust and bake for 45 to 60 minutes in a 325-degree oven. The top should be lightly browned.

FRANK PERDUE'S DINNER WITH A SPECIAL FRIEND

Dinner with your best friend should be relaxed and intimate. At the same time, though, it should indicate to that special person his or her importance in your life. Something stylish and out of the ordinary is called for, and Frank Perdue's dinner is the answer.

Mr. Perdue is not only a chicken connoisseur, but his firm is the number one poultry company in the Northeast, bringing both attention and economic stability

The bonsai forest centerpiece says "longevity" and sets the mood for
a relaxing evening with a friend.
Antiques shown include a rosewood and teak table, ca. 1650, imported from China;
polychrome Chinese "tobacco leaf" plates, ca. 1795; a pair of Chinese porcelain shells,
ca. 1750; mixed-twist stemware, ca. 1760, from England; Chinese bamboo and cane
chairs, ca. 1790; a silver heart box made by Barent Ten Eyck (1725–1760), from
Albany, New York; and a glass decanter, ca. 1783.
Other pieces shown: Winterthur's reproduction eighteenth-century brass candlestick;
Winterthur's reproduction brass shell box originally made by William Whetcroft (1735–
1794) of Maryland; and silverware from Reed & Barton.

to the rich farming region of lower Delaware, Virginia, and Maryland's Eastern Shore. Mr. Perdue is also an active patron of the arts in Delaware. He is particularly fond of Wilmington's Grand Opera House, a stately historic structure located in the heart of the city. He is known, too, for supporting several local museums and arts organizations.

This patron of the arts has created a culinary work of art featuring Cornish Hens Scheherazade served with baby carrots, baby peas, pearl onions, and savory Curried Brown Rice Pilaf. Forbidden Fruit Soufflé, a soufflé baked in an apple, is a tempting finale to the meal.

Mr. Perdue's menu deserves an exotic setting, provided by this table with its "Eastern" flair. Colorful Chinese porcelain, lavishly carved rosewood furniture, and a precisely formed bonsai centerpiece set the mood for the dinner to come.

Serve at this dinner a spicy wine with a hint of exotic flavor. A zinfandel might be a good choice.

Menu

Cornish Hens Scheherazade

Curried Brown Rice Pilaf

Tender Hearts Salad

Forbidden Fruit Soufflé

Zinfandel

Cornish game hens are small birds consisting entirely of light meat. Their flavor is delicate, and their small size makes them a festive alternative to larger birds.

As with all poultry, be very careful in the storage and preparation of the meat. Be sure to refrigerate all uncooked poultry immediately upon purchase and use it within two days. If more time will pass before the poultry is used, overwrap its sealed package in foil, freezer paper, or plastic, and freeze it. Properly frozen, it may be kept for up to six months. Always thaw poultry in the refrigerator; do not leave it out on a counter or stove top to defrost!

Before stuffing and cooking game hens, rinse them inside and out and pat dry. Do not store stuffed cooked hens. If cooked hens are to be refrigerated, remove the stuffing and store separately to retard spoilage.

This recipe recommends a 22- to 28-ounce bird for each person. For those with less hearty appetites, half a hen may be in order.

CORNISH HENS SCHEHERAZADE

Number of Servings: 2

Preparation Time: 15–20 minutes, plus 30 minutes refrigeration time

Cooking Time: 60 minutes

INGREDIENTS:

2 fresh Perdue Cornish game hens (22–28 ounces each)
4 tablespoons fresh lemon juice (reserve rind)
2 teaspoons soybean oil
½ teaspoon ground ginger
½ teaspoon ground cumin
Freshly ground pepper to taste
Paprika to taste
4 whole cloves
2 small onions, halved
6 fresh or frozen baby carrots, lightly steamed
½ cup combined fresh or frozen baby peas and pearl onions, lightly steamed

DIRECTIONS:

Rinse hens inside and out, pat dry with paper towels, and place in large shallow bowl. In small bowl, combine lemon juice, oil, ginger, cumin, pepper, and paprika. Pour into and over Cornish hens. Cover and marinate in refrigerator 30 minutes or longer.

Preheat oven to 350 degrees. Stick cloves into onion halves. Place 2 onion halves and ¼ of the squeezed lemon rind inside each hen. Tie legs of each hen together and fold back its wings. Sprinkle hens with pepper and paprika. Roast about 60 minutes or until juices run clear with no trace of pink when thigh is pierced with a fork. Serve hens surrounded by vegetables and Curried Brown Rice Pilaf.

CURRIED BROWN RICE PILAF

Number of Servings: 2

Preparation Time: 10–15 minutes

Cooking Time: 45–55 minutes

INGREDIENTS:

1 teaspoon soybean oil
⅓ cup chopped onion
1 teaspoon curry powder
¼ teaspoon ground ginger
⅛ teaspoon ground cumin
⅛ teaspoon ground turmeric
Freshly ground black pepper to taste
Dash cayenne pepper
½ cup uncooked brown rice
1 tablespoon raisins (optional)
1 can (10 ounces) low-sodium chicken broth
½ cup water
1 tablespoon fresh chives, minced

DIRECTIONS:

Preheat oven to 350 degrees. Heat oil in small nonstick skillet over medium-low heat. Sauté onion and spices in hot oil for 2 to 3 minutes until onions are tender but not browned. Stir in rice and raisins; remove from heat and set aside.

In 2-quart ovenproof saucepan, over high heat, bring chicken broth and water to boil. Stir in rice mixture; cover and boil 5 minutes. Place covered saucepan in oven and continue to cook 45 to 50 minutes until rice is tender and liquid has been absorbed. To serve, toss pilaf with chives.

TENDER HEARTS SALAD

Number of Servings: 2

Preparation Time: 20 minutes

INGREDIENTS:

1 8-ounce can low-sodium fancy sliced beets
2 teaspoons cider vinegar
1 teaspoon Dijon mustard
1 tablespoon soybean oil
Freshly ground pepper to taste
Pinch ground cinnamon to taste
2 small heads Bibb or Boston lettuce with outer leaves removed
2 teaspoons snipped fresh or frozen chives

DIRECTIONS:

Drain beets, reserving 2 tablespoons liquid. Cut shapes out of beet slices using small cookie cutter or cardboard pattern. In small bowl, combine reserved beet liquid, vinegar, and mustard for dressing. Whisk in oil in a slow stream; season with pepper and cinnamon. Toss beets with dressing and set aside.

Trim base of each lettuce head, if necessary, so that it sits flat; gently spread leaves open like a flower. Carefully wash lettuce in cold water and pat dry with paper towels. On each of the two salad plates, place one lettuce head. Decoratively arrange beet shapes among the leaves. To serve, drizzle with dressing and sprinkle with chives.

FORBIDDEN FRUIT SOUFFLÉ

| Number of Servings: 2 |
| Preparation Time: 40–45 minutes |
| Cooking Time: 25–30 minutes |

INGREDIENTS:

> 2 large unblemished cooking/eating apples
> ½ lemon
> 1 cup unsweetened applesauce
> 2 teaspoons honey
> Ground cinnamon to taste
> Ground nutmeg to taste
> 2 tablespoons applejack or calvados, divided (optional)
> 1 large egg white
> Confectioners' sugar

DIRECTIONS:

Preheat oven to 375 degrees. Lightly grease baking dish. Wash apples and, if necessary, cut a thin slice off bottom of each apple to make it stand upright.

Cut a ½-inch slice off tops of apples. Using a small, sharp knife and a grapefruit spoon, hollow out apples, leaving shells ¼ inch thick. Rub inside and top edges of apple shells with lemon to keep them from discoloring.

In small heavy-bottomed saucepan over low heat, combine applesauce, honey, cinnamon, nutmeg, and 1 to 2 teaspoons applejack. Cook, stirring often, until heated through but not boiling. In small bowl, with mixer at high speed, beat egg white until stiff but not dry. Into medium-size mixing bowl, pour hot applesauce. Add half the egg white; fold in with a rubber or wooden spatula. Add remaining egg white and fold in gently.

Sprinkle inside of apple shells lightly with additional cinnamon and nutmeg. Place apple shells in prepared baking dish; carefully fill with applesauce mixture, doming the top. Bake in center of oven for 15 to 17 minutes or until soufflés have risen and are very lightly browned on top. Remove soufflés from oven and sprinkle lightly with confectioners' sugar. To flame soufflés, heat remaining applejack in small saucepan until barely warm. Using a long match, light applejack and pour over soufflés. Serve at once.

CHAPTER FIVE

Menus for Special Occasions

⸺⬥⸺

INDEPENDENCE DAY CELEBRATION
WITH LEE IACOCCA

*I*ndependence Day is one of Lee Iacocca's favorite holidays. Mr. Iacocca vividly recalls his parents' stories of seeing the Statue of Liberty as they arrived in New York harbor, immigrants from Italy.

Lee Iacocca's success with Chrysler is well known. Equally impressive are Mr. Iacocca's efforts to preserve America's heritage. As a labor of love, he helped raise the many millions of dollars needed to restore the Statue of Liberty to her full glory—just as his father and mother first saw her.

The Fourth of July is Lady Liberty's birthday, and Lee Iacocca's Independence Day feast celebrates this American event in the best Italian style. Italian Meatball Soup, made by Antoinette Iacocca just as she did when she first came to America, features veal meatballs in a hearty chicken and vegetable soup. This very special starter has been one of Mr. Iacocca's favorites since childhood. Antipasto with Marinated Mushrooms, spicy Shrimp Palermo, and Peach Cream complete this Old Country meal.

This festive dinner's setting shouts celebration even as it recognizes the nation's

---

Chinese porcelain with the "Declaration of Independence" pattern dates from the mid nineteenth century. The unusual shapes of the porcelain salt box and ladle are based on original Chinese designs. A European firing glass, usually a dram glass, ca. 1775, is for the wine. The English lead ogee-bowled glass, ca. 1745, with a unique series of air twists in the stem, makes a perfect water glass. The set of eight silver knives, crafted in Baltimore, ca. 1828, by Andrew E. Warner, demonstrates the elegant simplicity of the traditional American flat-leaf motif. The silver forks and matching spoons, also American, date from the late eighteenth century.

history. Porcelain made in China to commemorate America's centennial depicts the signing of the Declaration of Independence. The swirling stems of the glassware remind us of Independence Day fireworks; streamers of bright ribbon in red, white, and blue and a scattering of glass stars evoke images of Old Glory flapping in the breeze. Provide sparklers for each guest to add more magic to the night.

Serve this rich Italian meal with a full-bodied but "rough" red wine. Chianti or another spicy Italian wine will do nicely. Rich, dark espresso with a twist of lemon is a must for topping off this feast.

Menu

Antipasto with Marinated Mushrooms

Italian Meatball Soup

Shrimp Palermo

Italian Bread with Sweet Butter ‡

Peach Cream

Chianti

Espresso

‡ (recipe not included)

PREPARATION TIPS: ANTIPASTO

Antipasto is—literally—a dish served "before the pasta." It can range from an appetizer or salad course to a full dinner, depending on the ingredients included on the antipasto platter.

Most antipastos are a combination of meats, marinated and fresh vegetables, cheeses, and, occasionally, fruits, served with warm, crusty bread. Among the traditional elements of antipasto are proscuitto, pepperoni, cappicola, hard salami, mozzarella cheese, provolone cheese, marinated mushrooms, roasted peppers, chickpeas, fresh tomatoes, black and green olives, and artichoke hearts. However, the scope of the platter need be limited only by the imagination.

Use the freshest ingredients available, marinating vegetables and slicing meats and cheeses at home if time permits. Cut or roll all ingredients so that they are easily managed finger foods; strips of pepper, thin slices of tomato, and rolls of meats and cheeses are much more palatable than large chunks. Serve the finest quality olive oil and vinegar as a dressing on the side; let guests add their own to taste.

Antipasto does not have to be limited to one platter. Use as many as are needed to accommodate the guests. Make sure not to limit the platters to one or two ingredients, and mix foods on them for color and variety of taste.

ANTIPASTO WITH MARINATED MUSHROOMS

Number of Servings: 6

Preparation Time: 25 minutes

INGREDIENTS:

Lettuce leaves (iceberg, romaine, or endive)
12 slices provolone cheese, rolled
12 slices Italian ham, rolled
12 slices mozzarella cheese, sliced
12 slices Genoa salami, rolled
3 eggs, hard-boiled and quartered
2 tomatoes, sliced into wedges
3 hot peppers, thinly sliced and seeded

1 sweet green pepper, sliced
Black olives and anchovy fillets as garnish

DIRECTIONS:

Line a plate with lettuce leaves and arrange cheeses and meats attractively. Add eggs, tomatoes, and peppers, and place olives and anchovies on top. Serve with marinated mushrooms on the side.

❖

MARINATED MUSHROOMS

Number of Servings: 6

Preparation Time: 20 minutes

Cooking Time: 5 minutes, plus 2 hours refrigeration

INGREDIENTS:

1 pound small mushrooms
¾ cup vegetable oil
¾ cup raspberry vinegar
1 tablespoon lemon juice
¼ cup parsley, freshly chopped
1 tablespoon oregano
Salt and pepper
1 clove crushed garlic

DIRECTIONS:

Clean mushrooms and remove stems. Set stems aside for some other dish. Combine all ingredients except mushrooms in a large pot and bring to a boil. Add mushrooms and turn heat off. Allow to cool. Mix well and chill for several hours or overnight.

ITALIAN MEATBALL SOUP

Number of Servings: 10

Preparation Time: 20 minutes

Cooking Time: 2 hours

INGREDIENTS:

1 stewing chicken or large fryer, about 4 pounds
1 medium onion, quartered
1 large carrot, cut in chunks
1 large rib of celery, cut in chunks
Cold water
Salt and freshly ground pepper to taste
1 pound finely ground lean veal
1 large egg
1½ tablespoons Parmesan cheese, grated
1 tablespoon fresh parsley
½ pound small pasta squares
Additional Parmesan cheese

DIRECTIONS:

In large soup kettle or pot, combine chicken, onion, carrot, and celery. Cover with cold water and bring to a boil. Season with salt and pepper to taste, and simmer for about 2 hours, until stock is reduced and chicken is very tender. Remove chicken. Strain stock into large bowl. Skim off most of the fat on top of the stock. Remove chicken from bones, and shred enough chicken to make one cup. Add to stock. (Save remaining chicken for another recipe.)

In medium bowl, combine veal, egg, Parmesan cheese, and parsley; mix thoroughly and form into tiny meatballs about the size of a large marble.

Return de-fatted stock to pot and bring to a boil. Drop in meatballs and pasta squares and simmer 20 minutes. Ladle into soup bowls and sprinkle with grated Parmesan.

SHRIMP PALERMO

Number of Servings: 6

Preparation Time: 10 *minutes*

Cooking Time: 20 *minutes*

INGREDIENTS:

    1 cup green onions, including tops, chopped
    2 cloves garlic, minced
    6 tablespoons butter
    4 cups fettuccine noodles, cooked
    1½ cups fresh whipping cream
    1 pound medium shrimp (cooked and shelled)
    ½ pound hot ground sausage (pre-cooked)
    2 cups Parmesan cheese, grated
    Salt and pepper

DIRECTIONS:

Cook green onions and garlic in 2 tablespoons butter until onions are limp. Set aside and keep warm.

Just before serving, place hot cooked noodles and cream in attractive serving dish that can be used over direct heat. Stir mixture over medium heat until the cream reaches the boiling point.

Immediately add onion, 4 tablespoons butter, shrimp, and sausage to the noodles. With two forks, toss the mixture vigorously and sprinkle with Parmesan cheese. Continue lifting and mixing until well coated. Season with salt and pepper. Pass additional Parmesan cheese to sprinkle over individual servings.

❖

PEACH CREAM

Number of Servings: 6

Preparation Time: 10 *minutes*

Cooking Time: 30 *minutes*

INGREDIENTS:

    1 tablespoon gelatin
    3 tablespoons warm water
    1 can peaches (no. 2 size), drained
    2 tablespoons lemon juice
    ⅓ cup sugar
    1½ cups heavy cream
    Mint leaves

DIRECTIONS:

Soften gelatin in warm water; place over hot water and stir until dissolved. Force peaches through sieve. Add gelatin, lemon juice, and sugar. Chill for 30 minutes. Whip the cream and fold into peach mixture. Pour into mold or individual serving dishes and chill. Garnish with mint leaves.

KEN KERCHEVAL'S UNTRADITIONAL
TRADITIONAL THANKSGIVING DINNER

*T*raditional Thanksgiving dinner takes an untraditional turn when served by actor-collector Ken Kercheval. Although best known as oilman Cliff Barnes on the popular television series "Dallas," Mr. Kercheval is also making a name for himself as a collector and dealer of Americana and the owner of the Los Angeles antiques shop The Glass Menagerie. His love of antiques and "country" furnishings enhances his up-to-the-minute entertaining style.

All the old favorites are included in this Thanksgiving dinner, but each dish is given a new twist, bringing a modern perspective to the holiday meal. Even venerable Tom Turkey takes on a new taste with a savory Ham-and-Cornbread Stuffing. The cornucopia, symbol of plenty, is presented here as a Frozen Fruit Salad replete with fruit and nuts. Dessert is turned over in an Upside-Down Apple Pie accompanied by Homemade Vanilla Ice Cream.

Perhaps the most unexpected and original dish comes from the most customary of Thanksgiving foods. Corn, which helped the settlers survive their first years in the New World, is served here in a unique and delicious Popcorn Soufflé with Fresh Cranberry Sauce.

The setting for this holiday feast is a bit more "early American" than the menu. Tin-glazed earthenware plates and horn-handled cutlery are handsome yet homey in appeal. With its woven plaid napkins and heavy earthenware salts and figurines, the table looks special yet comfortable, its country air a reminder of holidays past. An informal arrangement of fall flowers in a hollowed-out pumpkin as well as accents of colorful dried corn and gourds bring to mind the purpose of Thanksgiving, to celebrate the bountiful harvest.

Serve this dinner with a full-bodied red wine, such as a Chardonnay, which stands up to the savory blends of spices in stuffings and side dishes. For guests who prefer a nonalcoholic beverage, provide ice-cold spiced apple cider.

The Flock Room at Winterthur is filled with tradition. The woodwork (ca. 1715) from Morattico Hall, in Virginia, and the furniture in the William and Mary style suggest a sense of permanence. The tin-glazed earthenware plates, ca. 1698, from England, set the stage for a perfect Thanksgiving feast.
Other antiques shown include staghorn-handled flatware, ca. 1750, made in the United States; a petal-shaped earthenware salt, ca. 1630, with a white tin glaze, from Italy; a hard-paste figurine, ca. 1700, from China; a Chinese earthenware with tin-enamel-glaze knife rest, ca. 1730, from Europe; and glasses, from the middle to late eighteenth century.

Menu

Hot Deviled Eggs

Squash Vegetable Soup

Frozen Fruit Salad

Roast Tom Turkey with Ham and Cornbread Stuffing

Ken Kercheval's Popcorn Soufflé with Fresh Cranberry Sauce

Upside-down Apple Pie with Homemade Ice Cream

California Chardonnay

PREPARATION TIPS: POPCORN

Corn has been a staple of the American diet since this country's earliest days, and popcorn has been a favorite snack food almost as long. Recently, popcorn has developed a certain mystique, and several varieties of "gourmet" popping corn and seasonings have been introduced on the market.

Corn for popping should be stored, covered, in the refrigerator until use. Allow the corn to warm a bit, almost to room temperature, before popping. If popping in oil, follow the suggested proportions or use about one tablespoon of oil for each ¼ cup of popcorn. Be sure to let the oil heat thoroughly before adding the corn. To determine if the oil is hot enough, place two or three kernels in the heating oil. When they pop, add the remaining corn. If an air-popper is used, no oil is needed. If air-popped corn is unsalted and unbuttered, virtually no fat or cholesterol is added, making popcorn one of the lowest-calorie and most nutritious snack foods around.

For those who prefer popcorn slathered in butter and salt, several other flavorings might appeal. Try Mexican popcorn with grated cheese, salt, butter, and a touch of taco seasoning. Old Bay Seasoning, used for peppered crabs, is also a wonderful popcorn topping with butter. Parmesan cheese and garlic salt give popcorn an Italian flavor. Cinnamon, sugar, and butter make popcorn a grand *sweet* snack. Seasoned popcorn makes an interesting addition to soups and salads. The rule—try anything that sounds edible. The results may be surprising!

HOT DEVILED EGGS

Number of Servings: 10

Preparation Time: 20 minutes

Cooking Time: 10 minutes

INGREDIENTS:

10 eggs
2 small jalapeño peppers, cut into tiny pieces
¼ cup celery, finely chopped
¼ cup onion, finely chopped
¼ cup pickle relish
3 green olives, finely chopped
⅛ cup mayonnaise
1 tablespoon Dijon mustard
Salt and pepper
Paprika

DIRECTIONS:

Place eggs in large saucepan; cover with water and bring to a boil. Turn heat off and let eggs set 10 minutes in the hot water. Drain. Run cool water over and peel. Slice lengthwise. Scoop yolks out.

In small bowl, combine egg yolks, jalapeño peppers, celery, onion, pickle relish, olives, mayonnaise, and mustard. Salt and pepper to taste. Either put egg yolk mixture into a pastry bag or use a spoon to fill egg white shells. Garnish with paprika.

SQUASH VEGETABLE SOUP

Number of Servings: 10

Preparation Time: 15 minutes

Cooking Time: 30 minutes

INGREDIENTS:

1 large onion, chopped
3 tablespoons butter or margarine
3 cups homemade or canned chicken broth
1 large potato, pared and diced
1 cup frozen yellow corn
2 medium carrots, peeled and sliced
1 stalk celery, sliced
1 16-ounce can white kidney beans, drained
2 cups acorn squash, cooked and mashed
½ teaspoon salt
½ teaspoon ground nutmeg
⅛ teaspoon white pepper
½ pint heavy or whipping cream

DIRECTIONS:

In a 3-quart saucepan over medium heat, sauté onions in hot butter or margarine for 5 minutes, stirring occasionally.

Add chicken broth and heat to boiling. Cover; add potato, corn, carrots, celery, and kidney beans, and cook over low heat until the vegetables are just tender—about 15 minutes.

Add squash, salt, nutmeg, and pepper. Over high heat, bring to a boil. Cover and reduce heat to low; cook 5 minutes. Stir in cream and heat through.

FROZEN FRUIT SALAD

Number of Servings: 8–10

Preparation Time: 15 minutes, plus 3 hours, 15 minutes chilling time

INGREDIENTS:

  1 3-ounce package orange gelatin
  Dash of salt
  1 cup boiling water
  1 8¾-ounce can pineapple tidbits
  ¼ cup lemon juice
  2 cups whipped topping
  ⅓ cup mayonnaise
  1 medium banana, sliced
  ¼ cup maraschino cherries
  ½ cup chopped celery
  ½ cup chopped walnuts
  Lettuce

DIRECTIONS:

Dissolve orange gelatin and salt in boiling water. Drain pineapple, measuring syrup and adding water to make ½ cup. Stir liquid and lemon juice into gelatin. Chill until slightly thickened (about 1 hour, 15 minutes).

Mix whipped topping with mayonnaise, fruits, celery, and nuts until blended. Next, blend in slightly thickened gelatin. Spoon into 8″ x 14″ loaf pan. Freeze until firm. Unmold and let stand at room temperature 30 minutes before slicing. Serve on bed of lettuce.

❖

ROAST TOM TURKEY WITH HAM AND CORNBREAD STUFFING

Number of Servings: 8–10

Preparation Time: 25 minutes

Cooking Time: 4 hours

INGREDIENTS:

  8- to 12-pound turkey
  4 tablespoons melted butter

  Stuffing
  5 slices bread, toasted
  1 cup celery, diced
  1 cup onion, chopped
  2 tablespoons butter
  2 eggs, beaten
  2 tablespoons parsley

  ¾ cup ham, diced
  3 cups cornbread, diced
  1 teaspoon poultry seasoning
  1 cup chicken broth

DIRECTIONS:

Cut toasted bread into cubes. In a skillet cook celery and onion in 2 tablespoons of butter till tender. In a mixing bowl, combine eggs, parsley, and ham. Add cornbread, bread cubes, and poultry seasoning, and toss lightly until well mixed. Pour chicken broth in and mix.

Rinse turkey and dry. Stuff with cornbread stuffing. Place turkey, breast side up, on a rack in a roasting pan. Brush the bird with melted butter. Insert meat thermometer in the center of the inside thigh, making sure the thermometer does not touch the bone. Cover legs with foil and roast bird at 350 degrees for about 3 hours, 15 minutes. Remove foil on legs and baste with pan drippings. Continue roasting. The bird is done when the meat thermometer reaches 185 degrees. Total cooking time: 4 hours.

✛

KEN KERCHEVAL'S POPCORN
SOUFFLÉ

Number of Servings: 8

Preparation Time: 10 minutes

Cooking Time: 30 minutes

INGREDIENTS:

4 eggs
1 small can creamed corn
Salt and pepper to taste
½ cup grated Parmesan cheese
1 cup popped Ken Kercheval Old Capitol Popcorn
1 tablespoon frozen butter, chopped
1 tablespoon fresh parsley, chopped
Cranberry sauce

DIRECTIONS:

Separate egg yolks and egg whites. Beat egg whites until very stiff with electric beater in mixing bowl. Beat egg yolks with creamed corn, salt and pepper, and Parmesan cheese until well mixed. Roll in stiff egg whites and mix gently until yolk mixture and egg whites are blended. Add popcorn and mix just enough to coat popcorn with egg mixture. Transfer to deep ovenproof baking dish, approximately 5 to 6 inches wide and 5 to 6 inches deep. Sprinkle chopped frozen butter and about a tablespoon of Parmesan cheese on top and garnish with sprinkles of fresh parsley. Place in preheated 450-degree oven and bake for 30 minutes or until popcorn rises to the top of soufflé and soufflé is a golden brown. Serve immediately with cranberry sauce.

UPSIDE-DOWN APPLE PIE

Number of Servings: 8

Preparation Time: 15 minutes

Cooking Time: 50 minutes

INGREDIENTS:

¼ cup butter
½ cup pecan halves
½ cup brown sugar
Plain pastry for a 2-crust 9-inch pie
6 large, tart apples, peeled, cored, and sliced
1 tablespoon lemon juice
½ cup sugar
1 tablespoon all-purpose flour
1 teaspoon ground cinnamon
1 teaspoon ground nutmeg
Dash of salt

DIRECTIONS:

Spread butter evenly over the bottom of a 9-inch pie plate. Press nuts, rounded side down, into butter on bottom of plate. Pat brown sugar evenly over nuts. Roll out pastry for bottom crust and place in pie plate over sugar and nuts.

Sprinkle apples with lemon juice. Combine flour, cinnamon, nutmeg, and dash of salt and toss with apples. Turn apple mixture into pie plate; spread evenly.

Roll out remaining pastry; fold in half and place over apples. Fold top edge under bottom edge, making a slightly raised edge. Prick top of the pie with fork. Bake at 400 degrees for 50 minutes.

Remove from oven; cool 5 minutes. Place serving plate atop pie; invert. Carefully remove pie plate. Serve warm or cool with homemade vanilla ice cream.

A TREE-TRIMMING PARTY

*W*hether long-standing family celebrations or ethnic customs, traditions are especially important at Christmastime. Seasonal music, once-a-year foods, and familiar ornaments and decorations can help make a holiday gathering special, leaving happy memories that will last for years. Visitors who experience "Yuletide at Winterthur," the museum's annual holiday tour, come away with memories and new "traditions" that they will adopt and adapt as their own. This tree-trimming party at Winterthur is a fine example of the introduction of early-American customs into a modern celebration, giving the party old-fashioned charm.

Country flavor abounds, from the food served the guests to the decorations that grace the room. Cookies cut in fantasy shapes—in the old Pennsylvania German style—hang in the window panes. A tree decked with cookies in the shape of toy horses, ceramic geese, fruit, and popcorn strings takes center stage in the comfortable setting. Antique toys add a delightful touch to the scene. Painted horses and unicorns, rag dolls, wooden soldiers, and even Noah's Ark are reminders of the wonder of a child's Christmas.

Amid this unusual plenty is an abundant meal of favorite yuletide recipes from *Yuletide at Winterthur* (Winterthur Museum, 1980). Beef stew with crusty bread will warm even the coldest carolers on Christmas Eve. Fruitcake and Chocolate Candied Orange Peels appeal to young and old alike. And Christmas joy will come early to those who sample the Special Eggnog and Wagner's Fish House Punch!

Fruits, nuts, and beverages are set out on a cloth-covered table for tree trimmers, friends, and revelers who stop by. Be sure to have a fruit punch for the younger decorators. Cranberry or raspberry juice mixed with fruit and sparkling water or ginger ale make a bright red concoction perfect for the season!

Menu

Beef Stew with Crusty Bread

Fruitcake

Wig Cookies

Chocolate Candied Orange Peel

Wagner's Fish House Punch

Special Eggnog

Quince Jelly

Preparation Tips: Punches

Punch is the perfect party drink because it is an excellent way to serve a large number of people. It certainly eliminates a great deal of worry and work. Punch need not be the tutti-frutti variety many of us imbibed as children. If cranberry, grapefruit, or another tart juice is used as the base, the punch will not be overly sweet.

As always, fresh foods are preferable to frozen or canned, and juices are no exception. However, it is often difficult to obtain the large quantity of fresh juice needed for a punch. If using canned or frozen concentrated juices, try to get the unsweetened variety. Sugar or a sugar syrup can always be added later if more sweetness is desired.

Nonalcoholic punches can consist of almost anything. Juices mixed with ginger ale, sparkling water, or some other soft drink are among the most popular. Alcohol punch can be an expanded version of a popular drink, such as a daiquiri or planter's punch, or almost entirely made of alcohol, like Fish House Punch or Artillery Punch. Among the seasonal favorites at Christmas are wassail bowl and eggnog.

If serving a cold punch, chill the base before adding mixers or seltzer water. And be sure to keep the punch well chilled in its serving bowl. A large ice block, frozen in a gelatin mold or ring pan, is both decorative and practical. The ice takes a long time to melt, so it will not rapidly dilute the punch. Also, fruit or flowers can be frozen into the ice block, adding color and charm.

Hand-cut cookies from patterns made in the second half of the nineteenth century decorate the windows of the Kershner Parlor at Winterthur. The room, taken from a house built in 1755, in Wernersville, Pennsylvania, is a perfect place to celebrate the Yuletide season. Green feather-edged plates, made in the early nineteenth century by Enoch Wood & Sons of England, are on the walnut dining table, 1750–1800 (whose sawn X-shaped supports are the source of its modern-day counterpart, the sawbuck table).
Antique toys shown include a wooden horse pull toy, ca. 1840; a miniature side chair, ca. 1800; a spruce Noah's Ark, ca. 1840, complete with one hundred and fourteen animals and four carved figurines; toy wooden oxen, ca. 1850; a pine whirligig, ca. 1825; a chalkware cat, ca. 1850; and spotted wooden horse, ca. 1850.
Other objects shown include modern white porcelain cups and a porcelain punch bowl from Mottahedeh.

BEEF STEW

Number of Servings: 6

Preparation Time: 15 minutes

Cooking Time: 2 hours, 30 minutes

INGREDIENTS:

2 pounds boneless stewing beef, cut into cubes
½ cup flour
2 tablespoons butter
1 cup red wine
2 cups water
1 clove garlic, pressed
½ teaspoon sugar
½ teaspoon salt
¼ teaspoon freshly ground pepper
Pinch of ground cloves
6 carrots, peeled and chopped
2 onions, quartered
3 turnips, peeled and diced
Crusty bread
Horseradish

DIRECTIONS:

Coat meat with flour and brown lightly in butter. Combine wine and water with garlic, sugar, and salt, and bring to a boil. Pour over meat. Add pepper and cloves and stir. Simmer for about 1 hour and 30 minutes to 2 hours. Add carrots, onions, and turnips and continue cooking until vegetables are tender. Serve with crusty bread and horseradish.

Adapted from Mary Randolph, *The Virginia House-Wife*, 1830.

FRUITCAKE

Number of Servings: 12

Preparation Time: 45 minutes

Cooking Time: 3 hours

INGREDIENTS:

1 cup butter
1 cup sugar
5 eggs
1¼ cups orange juice
1½ teaspoons vanilla
3 cups flour, sifted
2 teaspoons baking powder
¼ teaspoon salt
1 pound raisins
1 pound candied cherries
1 pound candied pineapple
½ pound currants
½ pound citron
½ pound chopped nuts
½ pound candied lemon peel
½ pound candied orange peel
1 cup brandy

DIRECTIONS:

Cream butter and sugar. Add eggs, one at a time, juice, and vanilla. Mix in flour, baking powder, and salt. Add fruits and nuts. Let batter rest for about 30 minutes. Grease 10-inch tube pan. Line both bottom and sides with wax paper; grease and flour pan. Pour batter into pan and bake at 250 degrees for 3 hours. Remove cake from oven and cool. Remove cake from pan and place in a covered tin lined with cheesecloth. Pour on brandy, and wrap cloth over cake. Cover and store for several days. Check cake; if too dry, add more brandy. Makes a 5- to 6-pound cake. Adapted from *The American Housewife*, 1841.

WIG COOKIES

Yield: 3 dozen

Preparation Time: 4 hours

Cooking Time: 20 minutes

INGREDIENTS:

  1 package dry yeast
  ¼ cup warm water
  1½ cups warm milk
  6 cups flour
  1½ teaspoons salt
  1 egg, beaten
  ¾ cup sugar
  ½ cup butter, softened
  1 tablespoon caraway seeds
  ¼ teaspoon nutmeg
  Pinch of ground cloves
  Pinch of mace

DIRECTIONS:

Add yeast to warm water. When dissolved, add milk. Sift flour and salt into liquid and stir until blended. Mix in egg, sugar, butter, seeds, and spices. Cover bowl, put in a warm place free from drafts, and let double in bulk. Stir down and add enough flour to make a kneadable dough. Turn out onto floured board and knead for about 5 minutes. Place in a greased bowl, cover, and let double in bulk again. Punch down and turn out onto floured board. Roll out to ¼- to ½-inch thickness. Cut into wedges or whatever shape is desired. Place on greased baking sheets. Bake at 375 degrees for about 20 minutes or until lightly browned.
Adapted from E. Smith, *The Compleat Housewife*, 1742.

CHOCOLATE CANDIED ORANGE PEEL

Number of Servings: 6

Preparation Time: 15 minutes

Cooking Time: 3 hours

INGREDIENTS:

  2 cups orange (or grapefruit, lemon, or lime) peel
  1½ cups corn syrup
  2 cups granulated sugar
  Semisweet chocolate

DIRECTIONS:

Wash fruit. Remove peel from each piece in quartered sections.

Cut peel into thin strips and cover with cold water. Boil for 30 minutes or until tender. Drain and repeat cold-water-to-boiling process 3 or 4 times. Drain completely, and pour corn syrup over fruit. Cook gently until peel is transparent. Drain excess syrup, roll each piece in sugar, and dry. Makes about 1 pound. May be coated with chocolate after drying.
Adapted from *The Compleat Housewife*, 1742.

WAGNER'S FISH HOUSE PUNCH

Number of Servings: 50

Preparation Time: 10 minutes

INGREDIENTS:

1 ⅓ pints lemon juice
3 pounds sugar
1 quart cognac
1 pint peach brandy
1 pint Jamaican rum

4 quarts water
Cracked ice

DIRECTIONS:

Mix all ingredients and pour over cracked ice.
From the Winterthur Archives.

✠

SPECIAL EGGNOG

Number of Servings: 8

Preparation Time: 10 minutes

INGREDIENTS:

6 eggs, separated
¾ cup sugar
2 cups heavy cream
2 cups milk
1 pint whiskey
1 ounce Jamaican rum
Nutmeg

DIRECTIONS:

In a large bowl, beat egg yolks with ½ cup sugar until light and fluffy. In another bowl, beat egg whites until stiff, gradually adding ¼ cup sugar. Fold egg whites into egg yolks. Stir in cream and milk. Add whiskey and rum and mix thoroughly. Chill. After placing in serving bowl, dust nutmeg over top.
Adapted from George Jirardey, *Manual of Domestic Economy*, 1841.

✠

QUINCE JELLY

Yield: 8 1-pint jars

Preparation Time: 20 minutes

Cooking Time: 40 minutes

INGREDIENTS:

About 3 pounds ripe quinces
4 ½ cups water

¼ cup strained lemon juice (2 lemons)
7 ½ cups (3 ¼ pounds) sugar
½ bottle Certo fruit pectin

DIRECTIONS:

Remove cores and blossom and stem ends from about 3 pounds fully ripe quinces. Do not peel. Grind or cut fine. Place in saucepan. Add 4½ cups water. Bring to a boil, then simmer, covered, for 15 minutes. Place in jelly bag; squeeze out juice. Measure 4 cups into a very large saucepan. Add lemon juice.

To the measured juice in saucepan, add the exact amount of sugar specified in the recipe. Mix well. Place over high heat and bring to a boil, stirring constantly. At once stir in Certo. Then bring to a full rolling boil and boil hard 1 minute, stirring constantly. Remove from heat, skim off foam with metal spoon, and pour quickly into glasses. Cover at once with ⅛ inch hot paraffin. Recipe from Mrs. Nicholas du Pont.

CHRISTMAS DINNER FROM THE WINTERTHUR ARCHIVES

Christmas at Winterthur has always been a special time, filled with the time-honored traditions that surround the sharing of precious hours, elaborate meals, and treasured gifts with family and friends. Several customs established when museum founder Henry Francis du Pont and his family lived at the estate are still carried out by the museum today as part of its "Yuletide at Winterthur" festivities.

Some of these customs include a majestic eighteen-foot lavishly decorated Christmas tree, which graces the glass-walled Conservatory at the north end of the museum building. Vibrant poinsettias and Jerusalem cherries are displayed with fragrant paperwhite narcissus in museum rooms to show early-American holiday celebrations.

Among the season's highlights at Winterthur while it was still the home of the du Ponts was a festive meal, which varied little from year to year. Terrapin soup was a favorite appetizer, and entrées included Baked Ham in Madeira Sauce and Stuffed Goose. The red and green of Apple and Celery Salad and fresh cranberry sauce added seasonal color. A fitting finale to the holiday dinner was steamed Plum Pudding with hard sauce.

Exquisite *famille rose* porcelain dishes imported from China in the eighteenth century grace the table today. Eighteenth-century cutlery with handles of green-colored ivory add a cheerful holiday note. Out-of-season flowers, including lilacs, roses, and snapdragons, are special jewels at the table's center. Crisp linen napkins are tied with brass ornaments, rather than with napkin rings. These become favors for the guests to take home.

Several wines go with the lavish meal. Serve the appetizers with a full-bodied white wine, such as a chardonnay. A pinot noir is appropriate with either entrée. Following dinner, brandy or cranberry cordials may be served with the coffee. For guests who prefer, cranberry juice is a tart accompaniment. For an especially festive touch, add a little sparkling water and make a cranberry juice spritzer.

Menu

Melon

Clear Soup

Terrapin

Baked Ham with Madeira Sauce and Browned Potatoes

Holiday Stuffed Goose

Cranberry Relish

Apple and Celery Salad

Cardoons in Hollandaise Sauce

Plum Pudding

Chardonnay

Pinot Noir

Brandy

Christmas, as we know it, is a great festive day. Traditionally, it was the beginning of yuletide, a period of celebration that culminated in Twelfth Night. Yuletide was an ancient festival celebrating the winter solstice, a time of eating, drinking, and merrymaking. Winterthur carries on the yuletide tradition by serving this wonderful holiday meal. Antiques shown include famille rose *Chinese export porcelain, ca. 1740; English flatware with green-colored ivory pistol handles, ca. 1800; an English lead glass fingerbowl, ca. 1875; a silver salver, ca. 1750, made by William Whetcroft of Annapolis, Maryland; a rare soft-paste porcelain cauliflower-shaped covered dish, ca. 1775, originating in Worcester, England; a portrait of John Purves, a military man and member of the first Congress of the province, and his wife, Anne Pritchard, ca. 1775, by Henry Benbridge. Other pieces shown include an eighteenth-century Winterthur reproduction "sunburst" decanter by Mottahedeh and brass ornaments tied to the napkins as favors.*

PREPARATION TIPS: SOUFFLÉ

Soufflés are temperamental and must be prepared and served with care. But do not be discouraged! A good soufflé is usually well worth a little extra time and effort.

A soufflé should be prepared just before mealtime. Egg whites allow the soufflé to rise and impart to it its lightness; as soon as the egg whites are added, the soufflé should be placed *carefully* in the oven. Once a soufflé is cooked, it will not hold its puff for very long and should be served immediately.

Cook any meats, vegetables, or fruits to be used in the soufflé prior to mixing them with the eggs. Be sure to blend all ingredients completely before folding them *lightly* into the dry egg whites.

Prepare a soufflé dish by greasing and then dusting it with flour. This not only will keep the soufflé from sticking, but also will provide it with a surface to "grip" as it rises. Depending on the type of soufflé, the dish can also be dusted with grated Parmesan or Romano cheese, although this may stick slightly to the dish.

Finally, while cooking the soufflé and after it is done, keep it away from drafts. *Do not* open the oven door during baking, no matter how strong the temptation. The change in temperature or the shutting of the oven door may cause the soufflé to fall.

CLEAR SOUP

Number of Servings: 12
Preparation Time: 10 minutes
Cooking Time: 25 minutes

INGREDIENTS:

8 quarts strong beef stock
8 egg whites
8 egg shells
8 tablespoons water

DIRECTIONS:

Take a good, strong stock and remove all fat from the surface. For each quart of stock, whip 1 egg yolk, 1 egg shell, and 1 tablespoon of water together. Pour mixture into saucepan containing the stock; place pan over the fire and heat the contents gradually, stirring often to prevent the egg from sticking to the bottom of the pan.

Allow the mixture to boil gently until the stock looks perfectly clear under the egg, which will rise and float to the surface in the form of a thick, white froth. Remove it and pour the soup into a folded towel laid in a colander set over an earthenware bowl, allowing the soup to run through without moving or squeezing the towel.

Soup should be clear in color. Season with salt if needed and serve very hot.

✣

TERRAPIN

Number of Servings: 12

Preparation Time: 1 hour, 30 minutes

Cooking Time: 1 hour

INGREDIENTS:

> 2 terrapins (3 pounds each)*
> ½ pound sweet butter
> Salt
> Pepper
> ½ cup sherry
> 3 hard-boiled egg yolks

DIRECTIONS:

For each terrapin cut head off and plunge the body into a pan of very cold water. Change water twice and thoroughly scrub the shell and body with a brush. Place the body into a kettle of unsalted boiling water. Boil the terrapin until the skin of the feet becomes white. Draw off the water and add fresh water and cook until the feet feel soft when pressed. The shell should part easily also. Remove the terrapin from the water and let cool on its back. Pry the flat plastron from the curved carapace. Separate the liver and the gall bladder, being careful not to break the gall bladder. Discard the gall bladder, sandbag, heart, tail, intestines, and white muscles inside. Remove the large bones and cut meat into ½-inch pieces.

Put butter in a large heavy saucepan on the stove and heat until the butter is very brown; add meat and let it come to a boil. Salt and pepper to taste. Just before serving, add sherry. Garnish with hard-boiled egg yolks rubbed with butter into small balls to represent terrapin eggs.

Note: Canned terrapin can be substituted for live terrapin, eliminating the first step.

BAKED HAM WITH MADEIRA SAUCE AND BROWNED POTATOES

Number of Servings: 12

Preparation Time: 20 minutes, plus 24 hours soaking time

Cooking Time: 3 hours, 20 minutes

INGREDIENTS:

    1 uncooked country ham (6 to 7 pounds)*
3 quarts clear beef broth
2 medium onions
4 carrots
3 shallots
2 cups Madeira wine
1¼ cups water
1 clove garlic
8 potatoes, peeled and each cut in half
1 tablespoon flour
2 tablespoons water
Pepper
1 tablespoon unsalted butter

DIRECTIONS:

Soak ham for 24 hours in cold water to remove excess salt. Change the water at least 3 times. Drain. Place ham in a large covered pot, cover with 3 quarts of cold clear broth, and bring to a boil. Cook for 1 hour, 30 minutes. Let ham cool in the stock, then drain it. Remove rind and excess fat. Reserve the fat.

Preheat oven to 450 degrees. Peel onions, carrots, and shallots. Slice onions and shallots very thin. Grate the carrots. Put a few pieces of the reserved fat from the ham into a clean casserole and heat until fat is melted. Add the vegetables and cook until soft.

Pour in Madeira wine and 1¼ cups water. Add crushed clove of garlic. Place ham in casserole. Place potato pieces into casserole. Reduce heat to 350 degrees. Put the casserole into the oven and cook for 2 hours, turning every 30 minutes so the ham will brown evenly. Baste with the sauce in pan. When the bone can be pulled out but still offers some resistance, the ham is done. Remove the ham and potatoes from the oven and cover with foil to keep warm. Strain the pan drippings into a saucepan over medium heat. Add 1 tablespoon of flour dissolved in 2 tablespoons of cold water. This will thicken the sauce. Pepper to taste. Remove from heat and add the butter. Beat well. Serve in a sauceboat with the ham and potatoes.

*Note: A prepared country ham can be used, eliminating the first step of soaking for 24 hours.

HOLIDAY STUFFED GOOSE

Number of Servings: 12

Preparation Time: 12 minutes, plus 12 hours soaking time

Cooking Time: 3 hours, 20 minutes

INGREDIENTS:

    1 oven-ready goose (10 pounds)

Stuffing
½ pound prunes

3 red apples
2 medium onions
3 tablespoons butter
½ cup dry red wine

¼ cup water
1 cup fresh bread crumbs
½ cup walnuts, chopped
3 tablespoons fresh parsley, chopped
2 eggs, beaten
2 tablespoons sugar
1 teaspoon cinnamon

DIRECTIONS:

Stuffing—The day before cooking, place the prunes in a bowl, cover with water, and let soak for 12 hours. Drain the prunes and remove the pits. Chop prunes into small bits. Peel and core 2 of the apples (reserve 1 for garnish). Chop into small bits. Peel and chop onions. Heat butter in a frying pan. Add the onions and cook until soft. Remove from heat and add wine and water.

In a large bowl, combine prunes, apples, bread crumbs, walnuts, and parsley with the onion mixture. Add the beaten eggs to help bind the mixture.

Goose Preparation—Wash the goose and dry thoroughly with a cloth. Stuff the goose with the prune mixture. Truss the goose to enclose stuffing. Prick the goose all over with the trussing needle. Put the goose on its side on a rack in a roasting pan. Place pan in oven preheated to 450 degrees and cook until goose has browned on all sides. Turn goose frequently and baste with the excess fat.

Remove from the oven and reduce temperature to 350 degrees. Pour off excess fat. Turn goose breast side up and continue cooking for approximately 2 hours, 30 minutes (or 15 minutes for every pound). Continue to pour off excess fat once or twice during the cooking.

To garnish, peel and core the remaining apple and slice it very thin. Coat the apple slices with sugar and cinnamon. Arrange slices by overlapping them on the breast of the goose, and brush with fat drippings. Return to the oven and cook for 15 minutes.

❖

CRANBERRY RELISH

Number of Servings: 12

Preparation Time: 10 minutes

Cooking Time: 30 minutes

INGREDIENTS:

4 cups fresh cranberries
1 cup seedless raisins
1¼ cups sugar
1 tablespoon cinnamon
2 teaspoons ginger
1 cup water
½ cup onion (1 medium), chopped
½ cup apple (1 medium), peeled and chopped
½ cup celery, thinly chopped

DIRECTIONS:

Combine cranberries, raisins, sugar, cinnamon, ginger, and water in a large saucepan. Heat and simmer for 15 minutes, or until the berries pop and the mixture thickens. Stir in onions, apple, and celery. Simmer for 15 to 30 minutes, or until thick. Chill. Can be served hot or cold to accompany poultry or ham.

❖

APPLE AND CELERY SALAD

Number of Servings: 12

Preparation Time: 15 minutes, plus 1 hour soaking time

INGREDIENTS:

4 bunches white celery hearts
1 cup golden raisins
2 heads Belgian lettuce
4 apples
2 tablespoons lemon juice
2 small onions

Dressing
1⅓ cups vegetable oil
1 cup cider vinegar
1 tablespoon prepared mustard
2 teaspoons sugar
Pepper

DIRECTIONS:

Salad Preparation—Wash and cut celery hearts into small bite-size pieces. Shred pieces into very thin strips without completely separating them at their base. Place in cold water for about one hour so they will curl. Soak raisins in warm water for about 30 minutes. Meanwhile, rinse and dry Belgian lettuce. Tear into bite-size pieces. Core, peel, and cut apples into bite-size pieces. Sprinkle apple pieces with the lemon juice so that they do not turn brown. Peel and thinly slice onions, separating the slices into rings.

Place drained raisins, celery, apples, onion, and lettuce in a salad bowl. Pour dressing on and mix. Serve at once.

Dressing Preparation—Combine all ingredients in a jar with a tight-fitting lid. Shake well. Can be chilled and served at any time.

CARDOONS IN HOLLANDAISE SAUCE

Number of Servings: 12

Preparation Time: 15 minutes

Cooking Time: 40 minutes

INGREDIENTS:

6 pounds cardoons
¼ cup lemon juice
½ cup flour
4 quarts water
2 tablespoons salt
2 tablespoons oil

Hollandaise Sauce
1 cup butter
½ cup hot water
8 egg yolks, at room temperature
4 tablespoons lemon juice
Salt
Pepper

DIRECTIONS:

Cardoons Preparation—Cut away outer stems and leaves and wash and dry the cardoons. Cut them into 3-inch lengths and sprinkle with the ¼ cup lemon juice to keep from browning. Toss and coat thoroughly.

Mix flour and ½ cup of the water in a cup. Put the mixture into a large saucepan with the rest of the water. Add salt and oil and bring to a boil. Add cardoons. Cook for about 30 minutes, or until tender. Drain and cover with hollandaise sauce.

Hollandaise Sauce—Melt butter on top of a double boiler over simmering water. Stir in hot water. Remove from heat. Add unbeaten egg yolks all at once. Beat with an electric mixer for about 2 minutes, or until mixture has about doubled. Stir in lemon juice; salt and pepper to taste.

Place over simmering water again and cook for 5 minutes or until thick. (Do not overheat; it can cause curdling.) Remove from heat and let stand for a few minutes. Makes about 4 cups. Pour the sauce over the cardoons or serve separately.

PLUM PUDDING

Number of Servings: 12–16

Preparation Time: 15 minutes

Cooking Time: 3 hours, 30 minutes

INGREDIENTS:

1 cup milk
4 slices stale bread, cubed
6 ounces suet, ground
1 cup brown sugar, packed
2 eggs, beaten
¼ cup brandy
1 teaspoon vanilla
2 cups raisins
1 cup currants
½ cup nuts, chopped
½ cup candied orange peel
1 cup flour
1 teaspoon baking soda
½ teaspoon salt
2 tablespoons cinnamon
1 teaspoon mace
1 teaspoon ground cloves
Hard sauce optional

DIRECTIONS:

Pour milk over bread and stir. Add suet, sugar, eggs, brandy, and vanilla, and mix completely. In a larger bowl, mix raisins, currants, nuts, and peel.

Sift flour, baking soda, and salt and combine with spices. Add to the fruit-and-nut mixture and blend. Add the bread-and-suet mixture and stir well. Pour pudding into a greased 2-quart mold (do not use tube or bundt pans or ring mold). Cover mold completely with foil, using string to secure. Put mold on a rack within a deep pot or dutch oven. Add boiling water to the pot to about an inch, cover, and steam the pudding for about 3 hours, 30 minutes. Be sure water level is maintained in pot. Remove mold and cool for about 15 to 20 minutes. Remove pudding from mold and place on serving plate. Serve with wine sauce or hard sauce of your choice.

Chandler Farms, a brick house in the Federal style, was built in 1804 and remained in the Chandler family until 1916, when it was sold to their neighbors the du Ponts. In 1958, Henry Francis du Pont, who founded the Winterthur Museum, designated the house as the residence of the museum director. Its stately dining room is beautifully furnished with pieces from Winterthur's reproduction program and is a perfect setting for a New Year's Eve dinner. The table is set with reproduction "Brandywine" porcelain, based on the classical revival motif of a Chinese export porcelain dinner service, ca. 1800.
Other items shown include a silver candelabra; silver salts with cobalt liners; rose-colored cut-glass stemware; and crystal wine and water glasses, all from the collection of Mrs. Zoë Graves, wife of the current director.

JUDITH JAMISON'S NEW YEAR'S EVE DINNER

*J*udith Jamison has been called the "goddess of modern dance." During her fifteen years with the Alvin Ailey Dance Theater, from 1965 to 1980, she exhibited her talents throughout the world, in dance roles created especially for her and on Broadway, where she had a lead role in *Sophisticated Ladies*.

Ms. Jamison also excels as a hostess. An accomplished chef who has operated her own successful pie-making business, Ms. Jamison feels that she draws on many of the same creative forces when she cooks as when she dances. A consultant to Hennessy cognac, Ms. Jamison has created some very special recipes, perfect for warming one up on a cold winter night and for celebrating a festive occasion like New Year's Eve. Chicken Charleston combines cognac in a savory blend of seasonings, including tarragon, Dijon mustard, and capers. A sweet butter blend featuring cognac and pecans provides a sinfully delicious topping for hot-from-the-oven biscuits. The pièce de résistance, Judith Jamison's "Extraordinary" Sweet Potato Pie, is enough to cancel any New Year's resolution.

This New Year's Eve dinner deserves to be served in style. Gilt-edged "Brandywine" porcelain, with its intricate grape decoration in vibrant plum, complements the colorful cut-crystal wine goblets. Antique silver candelabra add an extra holiday glow. The intimate table is placed in front of the fire for added warmth on a cold winter's night.

Serve this festive dinner with an excellent dry white wine, such as Pouilly-Fuissé or with a very dry champagne, if the holiday mood really strikes. The rich pie must be accompanied by strong coffee and followed, of course, by cognac.

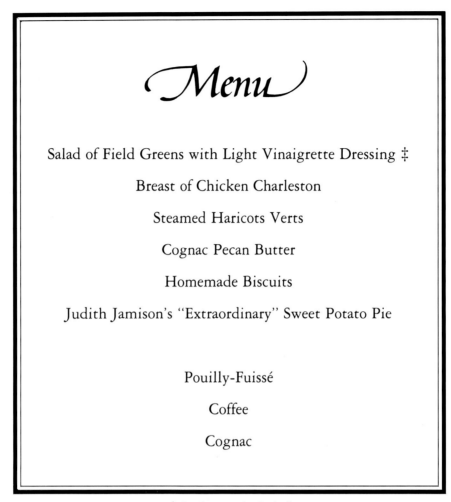

Menu

Salad of Field Greens with Light Vinaigrette Dressing ‡

Breast of Chicken Charleston

Steamed Haricots Verts

Cognac Pecan Butter

Homemade Biscuits

Judith Jamison's "Extraordinary" Sweet Potato Pie

Pouilly-Fuissé

Coffee

Cognac

‡ (recipe not included)

PREPARATION TIP: COOKING WITH SPIRITS

Wine, brandy, sherry, liqueurs, and other spirits can indeed add *spirit* to many dishes, as well as flavor and color. There are no firm and fast rules dictating which spirits are appropriate for use in cooking. The main consideration should be whether or not the particular wine or liquor used complements the other ingredients in the dish.

Always use wines or liquors that are "table" quality—that is, good enough to drink by themselves. They need not be the *most* expensive but should be of better quality than cooking sherry. One idea is to combine leftover bottles of wine and refrigerate them. This "house blend" will keep for quite some time and is remarkably good when added to foods.

Liqueurs are often most appropriate when added to desserts, and they are particularly wonderful with fresh fruits and ice cream. Sherry and cognac have any number of uses—in soups, aspics, butters, and, of course, desserts. Dry wines find their way into the largest number of cooked foods, including meat, fish, gravies, sauces, vegetables, dips and cheese blends, soups, and stews. Previously relegated to the more everyday dishes, beer is becoming more popular in a variety of more exotic dishes as well. Rum and bourbon are especially popular in cakes, cookies, and trifles.

When cooking with spirits, remember that they are liquids and should be included in the total liquid measurement of a dish. If adding wine or liquor that is not included in a recipe, be sure to eliminate some other liquid from the dish. The inverse is also true. If deleting liquor from a recipe, replace it with another liquid. Also, if spirits are added and then simmered, the alcohol will cook out, leaving only the flavor. However, if cooked too long, spirits lose some of their flavor as well. In many dishes, small amounts of spirits can be added for flavor just before serving.

BREAST OF CHICKEN CHARLESTON

Number of Servings: 8

Preparation Time: 10 minutes

Cooking Time: 35 minutes

INGREDIENTS:

8 chicken breasts, skinned and boned
1 cup flour
2 tablespoons dried tarragon
2 teaspoons salt
2 tablespoons unsalted butter
1 cup Hennessy v.s cognac
1 cup chicken broth
8 tablespoons Dijon mustard
4 tablespoons lemon juice
8 tablespoons capers

DIRECTIONS:

Split the chicken breasts lengthwise.

On a sheet of wax paper, combine flour, tarragon, and salt. Lightly dredge chicken breasts in the mixture, shaking off the excess.

In a large skillet, melt butter over moderate heat. Add chicken and sauté for 10 to 14 minutes, or until lightly browned on each side.

In a small saucepan set over moderate heat, warm the cognac. Pour it over the chicken and ignite, shaking the pan constantly until the flames subside. Add the chicken broth, mustard, and lemon juice. Cover the skillet, reduce the heat to low, and simmer for 20 minutes, turning the chicken breasts once.

Arrange the chicken breasts on a warmed platter. Using a fine sieve, strain the sauce over the chicken and sprinkle with the capers.

STEAMED HARICOTS VERTS (GREEN BEANS)

Number of Servings: 6	
Preparation Time: 10 minutes	
Cooking Time: 15 minutes	

INGREDIENTS:

1½ pounds fresh green beans
1½ cups boiling water
4 tablespoons butter

DIRECTIONS:

Wash and trim ends off of beans. To steam, cover beans in a bamboo steamer and place in a wok over medium heat. Carefully pour 1½ cups boiling water into the wok. This amount of water will produce steam for about 20 minutes. Cook 15 minutes for a crunchy bean, 20 to 25 minutes for a well-done bean.

Place in serving dish, add butter, and toss until beans are well-coated.

JUDITH JAMISON'S ''EXTRAORDINARY'' SWEET POTATO PIE

Number of Servings: 10	
Preparation Time: 1 hour	
Cooking Time: 55 minutes	

INGREDIENTS:

Crust
2 cups all-purpose flour
¼ teaspoon salt
12 tablespoons (¾ cup) cold shortening
5–6 tablespoons ice water, approximately

Filling
¼ cup dark raisins
¼ cup Hennessy v.s cognac
1 pound (about 2 large) sweet potatoes, peeled and cut into large chunks
4 tablespoons (½ stick) butter, softened
½ cup granulated sugar
3 large eggs, separated
½ cup evaporated milk

1 8¼-ounce can crushed pineapple in heavy syrup, drained, reserving 1 tablespoon of syrup
¾ teaspoon ground cinnamon
⅛ teaspoon grated nutmeg
1½ cups miniature marshmallows

DIRECTIONS:

Crust—Sift flour and salt together into a medium bowl. Cut in the shortening with a pastry blender until the mixture resembles coarse meal. Add water until dough holds together. Gather into a thick disc, wrap, and chill for at least 1 hour. Roll out into a 10-inch pie pan, fluting edges. Prick dough all over with the tines of a fork. Wrap and chill for 30 minutes. Preheat oven to 400 degrees. Bake pie dough for 10 minutes, or until light beige.

Remove pie shell from oven. Reduce oven temperature to 350 degrees.

Filling—Soak raisins in cognac for 1 hour to plump. Cook sweet potatoes in lightly salted water for about 15 minutes, until very soft. Drain well. Blend sweet potatoes with butter until just mashed. Do not mash completely smooth. Mix in sugar. Beat egg yolks lightly; stir into sweet potatoes. Stir in raisins with their cognac, evaporated milk, pineapple, pineapple syrup, cin- namon, and nutmeg. Beat egg whites until stiff, but not dry. Fold whites into sweet potatoes. Pour into crust and bake at 350 degrees for 40 minutes, until a knife inserted in the center comes out clean.

Remove pie from oven. Distribute marshmallows over top of pie, pressing lightly into filling to adhere. Return pie to oven and bake for 5 minutes until marshmallows are melted and lightly browned. Serve warm or chilled.

✤

COGNAC PECAN BUTTER

Number of Servings: 8

Preparation Time: 10 minutes

INGREDIENTS:

    1 ½ cups pecans
    1 stick unsalted butter, slightly softened
    4 tablespoons superfine sugar
    3 tablespoons Hennessy v.s cognac

DIRECTIONS:

Pulverize pecans in food processor or blender. Add butter and sugar, mixing well. Slowly add cognac to the mixture. Put mix- ture on wax paper and form into a sausage shape. Store in freezer.

✤

HOMEMADE BISCUITS

Yield: 2 dozen biscuits

Preparation Time: 15 minutes

Cooking Time: 12 minutes

INGREDIENTS:

    2 cups all-purpose flour, sifted
    ½ teaspoon salt
    2 teaspoons baking powder
    4 tablespoons butter, cold
    ¾ cup heavy cream

DIRECTIONS:

Preheat oven to 450 degrees. Sift flour, salt, and baking powder together. Cut cold butter into pieces. Cut in butter pieces until the mixture resembles coarse crumbs. Make a well in the center and add cream all at once. Stir until dough clings together.

Knead the dough once or twice and roll it out ¼ inch thick on lightly floured board. Cut into 2-inch rounds and bake on an oiled baking sheet for 12 to 15 minutes, or until golden brown. Serve warm.

VALENTINE'S DAY DINNER WITH
GHIRARDELLI CHOCOLATE

What says Valentine's Day better than chocolate? Nothing, especially when you are Dennis DeDomenico of San Francisco's renowned Ghirardelli Chocolate Company! The general manager of Ghirardelli is an antique collector as well as a connoisseur of fine chocolate.

This unique menu features chocolate in every dish, from the Brie Truffles appetizer to the sinfully delicious Zin-Sin Chocolate Mousse. Since colonial days, when a cup of hot chocolate was a morning luxury, chocolate has been one of America's favorite foods. Chocolate is still a luxury, given to sweethearts as a token of love, to children as a treat, to sick friends as a cheering-up gift, and to oneself as a small self-indulgence.

Not just *any* chocolate. This menu calls for delicious American chocolate from one of the country's oldest chocolate companies. Dark sweet chocolate is included in the dressing for the fresh orange and Cranberry Salad. Bittersweet chocolate is featured in the sauce for Moroccan Chicken. And half a pound of chocolate, as well as zinfandel, is the main ingredient of an incredibly rich Chocolate Mousse.

This heady meal is served at a richly set table. At each place is a Staffordshire plate from the mid nineteenth century. Small, jewellike fruit boxes, enameled in strawberry red and apple gold, add interest to each place, as do bisque cupids and other figures. The jewels, of course, are optional.

Serve this fabulous fantasy dinner with two wines. A spicy red, such as a zinfandel or a Côtes-du-Rhône, is the perfect accompaniment to the main course. A dry champagne is lovely with the Zin-Sin Chocolate Mousse.

Staffordshire earthenware transfer-printed plates, ca. 1847, show William Penn conversing with two Indians and are inscribed "W. PENN'S TREATY." The molded and cut glass from the early nineteenth century sparkles along with silverware sporting a shell-shaped handle, ca. 1800, made by Joseph Richardson, Jr. The cut-glass decanter, ca. 1820, from New York, is a perfect backdrop for the modern enamel boxes in fruit shapes. The white bisque porcelain angel from France, ca. 1890, accentuates the mood of the day.

Menu

Brie Truffles

Cranberry Salad Au Chocolat

Moroccan Chicken

Zin-Sin Chocolate Mousse

Côtes-du-Rhône

Champagne

PREPARATION TIPS: CHOCOLATE

Good chocolate should be stored and used carefully. Store chocolate in airtight containers at cool room temperature (ideally, about 65 degrees). Do not refrigerate or freeze it unless it would melt at room temperature. If chocolate becomes too warm, the cocoa butter melts and comes to the surface, causing a white "bloom." Although this makes it unattractive for eating out of hand, it does not harm the chocolate.

Chocolate burns easily and should be melted with care. The best method is to place the chocolate in a double boiler or in a bowl placed in a saucepan, over hot, but not bubbling, water. Another good way to melt chocolate is in a microwave oven on medium. If the chocolate does melt too quickly and becomes hard or grainy, add a little vegetable oil or margarine to the pan. This will smooth out the chocolate. Chocolate should melt at 100–110 degrees.

Strawberries are wonderful dipped in chocolate, as are dried apricots, pitted cherries, pear slices, orange sections, and bananas. For an easy and elegant dessert, melt semisweet chocolate carefully and let stand to thicken slightly. Then dip cookies—particularly macaroons, shortbread, oatmeal raisin, vanilla, or butter cookies—and let the chocolate harden in a cool place. Serve with fresh fruit or ice cream.

BRIE TRUFFLES

Yield: 24 balls

Preparation Time: 25 minutes, plus 4 hours chilling time

INGREDIENTS:

6 ounces Brie cheese
¼ cup unsalted butter, softened
2 ounces plain cream cheese, softened
1 tablespoon brandy
2 dashes cayenne pepper
½ cup walnuts, finely chopped
½ bar (4 sections) Ghirardelli bittersweet chocolate,
    finely chopped

DIRECTIONS:

Trim rind covering from cheese.

In small food processor, blender, or mixer, combine Brie and butter with cream cheese, brandy, and pepper. Mix until smooth and creamy. Stir in walnuts.

Chill overnight (or at least 4 hours) to blend flavors. Roll into 1-inch balls, about 1 teaspoon each.

Chocolate should be very finely chopped. A food processor is the easiest method. Roll cheese balls in chocolate for coating.

✛

CRANBERRY SALAD AU CHOCOLAT

Number of Servings: 6

Preparation Time: 15 minutes, plus 30 minutes chilling time

INGREDIENTS:

Salad
1-inch slice fresh orange
1½ cups fresh cranberries
⅓ cup sugar
2 tablespoons white zinfandel
1 head butter lettuce
½ bar (4 sections) Ghirardelli sweet dark chocolate,
    finely chopped

Dressing
⅓ cup light olive oil
3 tablespoons fumé blanc (or a dry light white wine)
2 tablespoons lemon juice
⅛ teaspoon salt
Pinch white pepper

DIRECTIONS:

Cut orange rind (zest) off orange slice; chop finely. Discard white part of rind. Cut fruit into pieces.

Cook cranberries, sugar, wine, and orange just until berries soften. (You may microwave, covered, 4 to 5 minutes on high.) Chill. Makes ¾ cup of relish.

To prepare dressing, mix oil with wine, lemon juice, salt, and pepper. Shake or stir until blended. Makes ⅔ cup dressing.

To set up salad, line individual plates with lettuce leaves. Mound cranberry relish in center. Pour some dressing over each salad. Garnish with chocolate.

✛

MOROCCAN CHICKEN

Number of Servings: 6

Preparation Time: 25 minutes

Cooking Time: 60 minutes

INGREDIENTS:

Chicken parts (3½ to 4 pounds)
2 tablespoons butter
1 tablespoon oil
1 cup long-grain white rice, parboiled
2 teaspoons curry powder
½ teaspoon ground cinnamon
1 cup hot water
16 ounces stewed tomatoes
½ cup dry vermouth
1 teaspoon salt
¼ teaspoon pepper
⅓ cup onions, chopped
⅓ cup almonds
⅓ cup raisins
½ bar (4 sections) Ghirardelli bittersweet chocolate, chopped

¼ cup chicken broth
Lemon wedges

DIRECTIONS:

In large skillet, brown chicken on skin side in melted butter and hot oil. Turn over chicken and stir rice between pieces of chicken. Mix curry and cinnamon with rice, heating a few minutes and stirring to coat rice with drippings. Add remaining ingredients, except chocolate, broth, and lemon in order given. Do not stir. Simmer, covered, 30 to 40 minutes or until chicken is tender and rice has absorbed all the liquid and is cooked. On a large platter, arrange chicken pieces around edge. Spoon rice into center.

To prepare sauce for chicken, melt chocolate in chicken broth. Drizzle over chicken. Serve with lemon wedges and mashed ripe avocado if desired.

❖

ZIN-SIN CHOCOLATE MOUSSE

Number of Servings: 6

Preparation Time: 20 minutes

Cooking Time: 20 minutes

INGREDIENTS:

2 bars (4 ounces each) Ghirardelli semisweet chocolate, broken
¼ cup butter
½ cup zinfandel

2 eggs
¾ cup whipping cream
2 tablespoons confectioners' sugar

DIRECTIONS:

In small heavy saucepan or a double boiler, melt, on low heat, broken chocolate with butter, stirring constantly. Add wine and continue heating and stirring until smooth. Remove from heat.

Slightly beat 1 whole egg with 1 yolk. Add quickly to chocolate mixture, stirring until thick. Beat remaining egg white until stiff peaks form. Fold into chocolate mixture. Whip cream with confectioners' sugar. Fold into chocolate mixture.

Pour into fancy stemmed glasses or chill and then use a pastry bag to pipe into glasses. Good served soft at room temperature or chilled to set firm.

LADY BIRD JOHNSON'S TEXAS FIESTA

*L*ady Bird Johnson impresses most folks as a woman of quiet dignity, with a keen sense of humor and a passion for beauty and nature. It is appropriate that she entertains outdoors—close to the landscape she loves—in a relaxed and casual way. At the L.B.J. Ranch, located in Stonewall, Texas, in the heart of the Texas hill country, Mrs. Johnson often gathers friends for a Mexican fiesta or a barbecue, meals reflecting the dual heritage of Texas.

At a barbecue harking back to early settler days, tables are covered with red-and-white checked cloths, and colorful bandanas are the napkins. Dinner is served on enameled tin plates and cups from an old chuck wagon.

The fiesta features colorful antique pottery set on vivid rugs covering a rustic wood table. Mrs. Johnson is very fond of wildflowers; if they are not available, Mexican straw flowers may be used to provide a casual, colorful focus for each table.

The fiesta menu features traditional Tex-Mex dishes, as well as Mrs. Johnson's personal favorites such as Buttermilk Sherbet with Fresh Pineapple, and Noche Specials. She comments: "'Noche Specials' announce to our guests that they are in the Southwest—a favorite snack with drinks in our part of the country." The word has spread from Texas, and noches, or nachos as they are more popularly known, have become an hors d'oeuvres staple from Paris, Texas, to Paris, France.

Serve this wonderful meal outdoors on a warm spring or summer evening and accompany it with Mexican beer and a pitcher of margaritas. For guests who prefer nonalcoholic beverages, serve well-iced limeade from freshly squeezed lime juice (with just a *hint* of lemon and *lots* of sugar).

A mixture of antique American and English earthenware is perfect for a "Texas fiesta."
Slipware decoration of red earthenware plates has been traditional in Europe since the
seventeenth century. Early pieces were usually village craftware. A favorite decorative feature
is the inscription of names using trailed slip. Typical colors are brown, black, and creamy
white. Methods of slipware decoration include painting with a full-bodied brush, trailing,
lining, feathering, resist, and stenciling.
Antiques shown include an English earthenware pitcher, ca. 1680; English earthenware
plates, ca. 1700–1775; English cruet stand, ca. 1700; American earthenware figure of a
chicken, ca. 1775.
Other items shown include an Indian rug, courtesy of Products of Great Import, and modern
black ironware plates. The yellow-handled flatware is from Reed & Barton.

Menu

Guacamole

Noche Specials

Chili Con Queso

Picadillo Meat Dip

Enchiladas

Pedernales River Chili

Buttermilk Sherbet with Fresh Pineapple

Mexican Beer

Limeade

PREPARATION TIPS: CHILI CON QUESO AND HOT PEPPERS

Chili con queso is a most versatile dish. It is included in this menu as a dip for corn or tortilla chips, but it can accompany almost anything. Mrs. Johnson suggests using it as stuffing for deviled eggs or celery hearts. It makes a terrific topping for hamburgers or hot dogs and is delicious spread on toast, crackers, or even in sandwiches. It can be used in omelets or on scrambled eggs. Be imaginative and create your own favorites.

Many Tex-Mex recipes include hot peppers, such as jalapeño or chili peppers. These tiny, unassuming vegetables can really pack a punch, so be careful in both their handling and use. Oils from the peppers can cause a burning sensation on the skin and are easily transferred to the eyes and mouth, where they can produce an extremely uncomfortable burn. Wear gloves when chopping peppers, or handle them with a dish towel.

Be sparing when using hot peppers as a spice. Most people, especially those new to Tex-Mex, prefer their food somewhere between mild and hot. Large doses of peppers can make a dish positively volcanic! If you wish, serve a small dish of fresh or roasted peppers as a condiment so that those who dare can add extra spice to their dinner.

GUACAMOLE

Yield: 1½–2 cups

Preparation Time: 20 minutes

INGREDIENTS:

3 ripe avocados
1 large tomato
1 chili pepper or Tabasco sauce to taste
2–3 green onions or scallions
Juice from 1 lemon, halved

DIRECTIONS:

In medium mixing bowl, mash pulp from the avocados with a silver fork, and combine it with the tomato, which has been peeled and seeded. Finely chop the chili pepper and green onions. Add to avocado mixture along with lemon juice. Mix thoroughly and serve with Noche Specials.

NOCHE SPECIALS

Number of Servings: 8

Preparation Time: 20 minutes

Cooking Time: 15 minutes

INGREDIENTS:

12 large round corn tortillas
Oil for frying
16 ounces cheddar cheese, grated
7–8 jalapeño peppers, sliced

DIRECTIONS:

Cut tortillas into quarters and fry in deep hot oil until brown and crisp on both sides. Drain on paper towels. Transfer tortillas onto a cookie sheet and put about 1 teaspoon grated cheese and a slice of jalapeño pepper on each quarter. Bake in a 350-degree oven until cheese begins to melt. Serve at once.

CHILI CON QUESO

Number of Servings: 1 ½ cups

Preparation Time: 5 minutes

Cooking Time: 15 minutes

INGREDIENTS:

    1 8-ounce can crushed tomatoes
    1–2 green chili peppers
    8 ounces pasteurized cheese

DIRECTIONS:

Combine tomatoes and chili peppers in a medium-size bowl. In a double boiler, melt the cheese. Add tomato mixture to cheese and blend well. Serve warm with corn tortillas.

Note: cheese must be pasteurized for this recipe to work.

PICADILLO MEAT DIP

Number of Servings: 8

Preparation Time: 15 minutes

Cooking Time: 40 minutes

INGREDIENTS:

    1 pound lean ground beef
    1 onion, chopped
    2 garlic cloves, pressed
    1 cup tomatoes
    1 tablespoon distilled vinegar
    ¼ teaspoon ground cumin
    1 teaspoon salt
    1 bay leaf
    ¼ teaspoon oregano

    2 jalapeño peppers, chopped
    ½ cup raisins
    ½ cup slivered almonds
    Taco chips

DIRECTIONS:

Cook meat in frying pan. When it begins to release fat, add both onions and garlic. When meat has browned, add all but raisins and almonds, and simmer 30 minutes. Add raisins and almonds. Simmer another 5 to 10 minutes. Serve hot with taco chips.

ENCHILADAS

Number of Servings: 12

Preparation Time: 10 minutes

Cooking Time: 15 minutes

INGREDIENTS:

12 corn tortillas
1 large onion, chopped
2 cups prepared chili
3 cups American cheese, shredded
1 cup chili juice

DIRECTIONS:

Fill a 2-quart pot about ¾ full of water; let come to a boil. Place tortillas, one at a time, in the hot pot of water for 1 second. Keep water hot.

Place ½ teaspoon onion, 2 tablespoons chili, and about 2 tablespoons shredded cheese on each tortilla, and fold or roll over. Place filled tortillas side by side in a baking dish. Pour chili juice over the enchiladas. Bake 10 to 12 minutes in a 350-degree oven.

Remove from oven and sprinkle with remaining shredded cheese. Return to oven and bake 5 minutes longer. Serve immediately.

❖

PEDERNALES RIVER CHILI

Number of Servings: 8

Preparation Time: 15 minutes

Cooking Time: 1½ hours

INGREDIENTS:

4 pounds coarsely ground round steak
1 large onion, chopped
2 cloves garlic, pressed
1 teaspoon ground oregano
1 teaspoon comino seed (cumin)
6 teaspoons chili powder or ¾ cup chili paste
1½ cups canned whole tomatoes
2–6 dashes hot sauce

Salt to taste
2 cups hot water

DIRECTIONS:

Place meat, onion, and garlic in a large, heavy frying pan or Dutch oven. Cook until light colored. Add oregano, comino seed, chili powder, tomatoes, hot sauce, salt, and hot water. Bring to boil, lower heat, and simmer for 1 hour. Skim off fat during cooking.

❖

Buttermilk Sherbet with Fresh Pineapple

Yield: 1 quart

Preparation Time: 45 minutes to 1 hour

INGREDIENTS:

1 quart buttermilk
½ cup sugar
2 tablespoons grated lemon rind
¼ cup lemon juice
1 ½ cups corn syrup (white)

⅛ teaspoon salt
2 cups crushed pineapple

DIRECTIONS:

Combine first six ingredients, then add well-drained pineapple. Mix. Freeze in an ice-cream freezer.

A WEDDING RECEPTION IN THE FINEST AMERICAN STYLE

*E*ddy Nicholson works as hard at his hobbies as he does at his career. The same drive that led him to develop Congoleum into a multimillion-dollar corporation helped him to acquire in just seven years one of this country's finest collections of early-American decorative arts. While encouraging world-record prices and media speculation, his quest for "the best" has resulted in the recent addition of several unparalleled pieces to his art collection. Mr. Nicholson recognizes quality, appreciates it, and chooses it for himself and his family.

A true connoisseur, Mr. Nicholson accepted only perfection for the recent wedding of his daughter. To create the wedding feast, Mr. Nicholson engaged Anton Mosimann, executive chef at London's Dorchester Hotel. He was recently cited as the "top chef" in the world by *Gourmet*. Five chefs from London and Canada assisted Chef Mosimann in preparing a truly remarkable wedding meal.

The wedding repast included such delicacies as Smoked Salmon rosettes filled with Trout Mousse, Chicken Consommé covered with puff pastry, Steamed Sea Bass with Red and Yellow Pepper Sauces, and chilled Fillet of Beef with "haystacks" of fresh vegetables. Three imported cheeses with walnut bread accompaniment were used to clean the palate before the desserts. Desserts included a Terrine of Oranges in a fresh Raspberry Sauce, delicate Petits Fours, and Black Truffles.

The pièce de résistance, as it should be, was the wedding cake, made especially by

Ron Fousek of the Four Seasons Pastry Shop in Boston. The five-tiered hazelnut torte, with mocha filling and white icing, was decorated with frosting replicas of the hand embroidered lily of the valley on the bridal dress.

This unsurpassed menu was served with wines to complement each course. A champagne, Laurent Perrier Champagne Brut Rosé, accompanied the wedding cake, along with many wishes of long life and continued happiness for the bride and groom.

Menu

1983 Gewürztraminer

"Réserve Personelle"

Hugel et Fils

1985 Montagny

Louis Latour

1979 Château Lascomber

Deuxeme Grand Cru de Margaux

1984 Muscat Beaumer de Venise

Paul Jaboulet

Demitasse

Coffee

Champagne Brut Rosé

Laurent Perrier

Menu

Smoked Salmon

with Trout Mousse Dorcester-Style

Chicken Consommé

with White Asparagus

and Black Truffles

Steamed Sea Bass

with Two Pepper Sauces

Poached Fillet of Beef

with Haystacks of Vegetable

Assortment of Cheeses

Terrine of Oranges

with Raspberry Sauce

Petits Fours ‡

Wedding Cake ‡

Menu and recipes by Chef Anton Moismann
‡ (recipe not included)

A table set to remember is the only way to describe this elegant fare. A centerpiece of Lady Diana roses surrounded by lush green ferns adds sparkle to the Chinese export porcelain, ca. 1790. The cornucopia crest design surrounded by a wide band of overglaze blue with gilt stars is borne by about a dozen families. The modern stemware is reflected in the 18-karat gold goblets, ca. 1920, made by Bailey, Banks & Biddle of Philadelphia.
Other items shown include eighteenth-century-pattern silverware from Reed & Barton, modern silver-topped salt and peppers, and antique napkins from a private collection.

Preparation Tip: Garnishing with Flowers

Fresh flowers have broken out of the centerpiece and have become acceptable, even desirable, for adding color to almost any dish. Whether included as an edible part of the meal, like peppery nasturtiums floated on soup or added to a summer salad, or used simply as a decoration, flowers can add interest, flair, and even flavor to a meal.

A wedding cake topped with fresh flowers is one of the most memorable events in the festivities. To echo the fresh-flower decoration, carry the design into the cake's icing. The Nicholson wedding cake had lilies of the valley at the base of the cake, and also on the top, a motif also seen in the bride's dress. Almost any flower in a bridal bouquet can be used to accent a wedding cake; roses, Peruvian lilies, lilacs, daisies, tuberoses, and orange blossoms make lovely alternatives to the traditional figures of a bride and groom.

Place flowers individually on dinner or serving plates or on the plates of hors d'oeuvres. One or two spiky spider mums make a dramatic centerpiece for a tray of sushi. Colorful squash or pumpkin flowers add whimsy to a platter of breads and cheeses. As always, the virtually limitless possibilities depend on individual taste and imagination.

Be sure to avoid toxic plants—or, at least, use them carefully. Poinsettias and holly, two Christmas favorites, are toxic if eaten. Flowers from vegetable plants are always safe and usually quite pretty and colorful. Also, many herbs are as delicate and decorative as flowers and are guaranteed to be edible!

When preparing flowers for garnishing, keep them fresh in a plastic bag in the refrigerator until needed. Be sure the flowers have not been sprayed with harmful pesticides, which can be as toxic as the most toxic plants. If using fresh-cut garden flowers, dip the heads quickly in cool water before refrigeration and carefully shake them dry onto a paper towel. This process will remove any unwanted ants, beetles, or other garden pests. If preparing flowers for eating, such as sugared violets, soak them well.

Smoked Salmon with Trout Mousse Dorchester-Style

Number of Servings: 12

Preparation Time: 20 minutes, plus 2 hours, 30 minutes, refrigeration

INGREDIENTS:

6 leaves of gelatin
2¼ ounces warm water
13½ ounces smoked trout fillet
2¼ ounces sherry
1½ ounces cognac
2 teaspoons fresh horseradish, finely grated
Salt and pepper, freshly ground
18 ounces whipping cream
24 thin slices Scottish smoked salmon

Garnish
12 leaves of Belgian endive
12 leaves red chicory
12 half-slices of cucumber
12 slices of hard-boiled egg (3 eggs)
12 slices of truffle
12 sprigs of parsley

DIRECTIONS:

Soften the gelatin in the warm water. Pour into a blender or food processor. Add the smoked trout and blend at top speed for a minute or two until the ingredients are pureed. Pour mixture into a large mixing bowl. Using an electric mixer, beat in the sherry, cognac, horseradish, and season to taste with salt and pepper. Overseason slightly, as the cream, which is added later, will mask the flavor a bit. Cover and chill until almost set, stirring occasionally.

In another bowl, beat the whipping cream until it doubles in volume and holds its shape softly. Gently fold the whipped cream into the chilled fish mixture. Pack the mousse into individual, lightly oiled molds. Cover with wax paper and chill for several hours before unmolding. The trout mousse is served on a salad-size plate with thin slices of smoked salmon overlapping in a rose petal fashion on a bed of endive and red chicory leaves. Garnish with half-slices of cucumber, slices of hard-boiled egg, slices of truffle, and a sprig of parsley.

Chicken Consommé with White Asparagus and Black Truffles

Number of Servings: 12

Preparation Time: 25 minutes

Cooking Time: 2 hours, 45 minutes

INGREDIENTS:

2 raw chicken carcasses (about 2 pounds)
2 onions with skins
7 pints water

1 clove
¼ bay leaf
1 medium leek, cleaned and roughly cut

½ stalk celery, roughly cut
Juice of one lemon

To Clarify
1 pound raw chicken leg meat, minced
3 egg whites, whisked until frothy
1 tomato, chopped
2 sprigs of fresh tarragon

Garnish
30 small tips of white asparagus, well blanched
30 thin slices of black truffle
30 sprigs of chervil

DIRECTIONS:

Blanch the chicken carcasses in boiling water for one minute. Remove and rinse the carcasses under cold running water. Halve the onions and place the cut sides down on a non-stick pan or broil cut side up until dark brown. Add all the ingredients for the stock to the pan. Bring to the boil, reduce heat, and simmer for 1½ hours. Strain through a fine cloth. Return to a clean pan.

To clarify the stock, stir together all the ingredients and whisk into the warm stock. Bring slowly to a boil, whisking all the time. When it comes to a boil, stop whisking, reduce heat, and simmer for 45 minutes. Line a sieve or colander with a fine cloth and spoon the froth into it. Pour the stock through this froth. It will be completely clear. Remove fat by dragging strips of paper towels over the surface of the consommé. Heat to serving temperature, spoon into soup plates, and garnish with asparagus tips, truffle slices, and tiny sprigs of chervil.

Note: The above can also be served in soup cups, covered in puff pastry and baked at 375 degrees for 15–17 minutes. The aroma released from this procedure is outstanding when the covering is broken.

⊕

FILLETS OF POACHED SEA BASS WITH TWO PEPPER SAUCES

Number of Servings: 12

Preparation Time: 10 minutes

Cooking Time: 20–30 minutes

INGREDIENTS:

6 large yellow peppers
6 large red peppers
3 shallots, finely chopped
6 small cloves of garlic, skinned and crushed
Few sprigs of thyme
4¾ quarts fish stock (plus 1¼ quarts for steaming)
12 sea bass fillets (5 ounces each)

DIRECTIONS:

Wash and trim peppers and cut into large pieces. Sweat shallots and garlic in non-stick frying pan over gentle heat without browning. Divide shallot mixture between two saucepans and add yellow peppers to one pan and red peppers to the other.

Divide the thyme and fish stock between the two pans. Cover and simmer for 15 minutes. Liquefy each mixture, strain, and season to taste with salt and pepper.

Season the fish and steam with remaining fish stock for 4–5 minutes, or until they flake easily with a fork. Arrange sauces on plates one on each side. Be sure to keep the line between sharp and definite. Top with fish and serve at once.

⊕

POACHED FILLET OF BEEF WITH HAYSTACKS OF VEGETABLES

Number of Servings: 12

Preparation Time: 35 minutes

Cooking Time: 12–15 minutes

INGREDIENTS:

12 ounces carrots, peeled, blanched
12 ounces courgettes, trimmed, blanched
12 ounces raw beetroot, peeled
12 ounces yellow pepper, trimmed, blanched
12 ounces celery, trimmed
12 ounces white radishes, trimmed
12 fillets of beef (5 ounces each)
Salt and freshly ground pepper
2¼ pints strong beef stock
12 tablespoons chives, cut in ½-inch lengths

Sauce
1½ cups reduced white chicken stock
6 tablespoons tarragon vinegar
6 teaspoons French mustard

DIRECTIONS:

Blanch the carrots, courgettes, yellow pepper, and celery separately. Drop into boiling, lightly salted water, then bring back to boiling. Remove vegetables and plunge into cold water. Keep covered at room temperature so they won't dry out. Cut all the vegetables into very fine julienne strips. Keep each vegetable separate.

Season the fillets with salt and pepper, then poach them a few at a time to make sure they are covered by the beef stock for 4–5 minutes. Remove the beef from the stock and cool. Reduce the stock to 1½ cups, then whisk in the vinegar, reduced white chicken stock, and mustard to make the sauce.

Moisten each pile of vegetables with a little of the sauce, reserving some for the beef. Season to taste. Arrange small mounds of each vegetable around the edge of each plate. Place the beef in the center, spoon over a little of the remaining sauce, and sprinkle with cut chives. Serve immediately.

✥

TERRINE OF ORANGES WITH RASPBERRY SAUCE

Number of Servings: 15

Preparation Time: 25 minutes, plus 3½ hours chilling time

INGREDIENTS:

18 medium oranges
2 cups clear apple juice
8 leaves gelatin, soaked in cold water and squeezed dry
1 bunch fresh mint leaves

8 teaspoons Grenadine syrup
½ cup water
Fresh raspberries
15 tiny mint sprigs for garnish

Raspberry Sauce
1 quart raspberries
1 tablespoon lemon juice
4 tablespoons confectioners' sugar

DIRECTIONS:

Pare the zest from 3 of the oranges, remove the white pith part and cut into thin julienne strips. Reserve. Squeeze the juice from these oranges (about 1¼ cups). Cut away the peel and white pith from all the remaining oranges, and carefully remove the orange segments. Remove seeds. Reserve the juice from the segmenting, add it to the other quantity, and strain it through a fine sieve (about 2½ cups).

Dissolve the gelatin in a little warm apple juice, then add to the remaining apple juice. Add ½ cup of the strained orange juice to the apple juice. Chill a 1½-quart terrine dish and spoon about ¼ inch of the apple juice and jellied mixture over the base. Chill until set; then overlap some mint leaves to cover the jellied mixture entirely.

Place the terrine in a large bowl of ice. Lay on one side and spoon a little apple juice, when firm repeat on the opposite side and press mint leaves into the juice. Chill until firm. Do this twice. Arrange half the orange segments on top of the mint leaves and spoon half the remaining juice over. Chill until set. Repeat the step above with the remaining orange segments and apple juice. Chill until set.

Raspberry Sauce—Using a food processor, make a puree of the raspberries. Reserve twelve berries for garnish. Strain the puree. Add sugar and lemon juice.

Assembly—Place chilled terrine in a dish of hot water for a few seconds to loosen the edges. Place serving plate on top of the terrine and invert. Spoon raspberry sauce on each serving plate and rotate to cover the bottom. Center a slice of the terrine in the sauce and garnish with a sprig of mint and fresh raspberry.

Approximately one thousand acres of rolling hills in naturalistic gardens at Winterthur are perfect for a coaching picnic. The stone wall of the Golf Barn is a perfect shelter for antique baskets, modern silver trays, and modern silver salt shakers. The reproduction silver Meyer Myers beakers, ca. 1760, are ready for the iced vodka. Point-to-Point race brochures record the day's activities.

214

CHAPTER SIX

Dining Out-of-Doors

—————————— ◆ ——————————

FROLIC WEYMOUTH'S PICNIC AT THE POINT-TO-POINT RACES

*M*ay in the Brandywine Valley is heralded by warmer weather, longer days, and glorious gardens in full bloom. In recent years, area residents have come to celebrate spring with an event fast becoming a Delaware institution—the Winterthur point-to-point race.

There have been point-to-point races in America since the nation's earliest days. The point-to-point race matches top race horses and jockeys against the course complete with jumps, obstacles, and sharp curves—rather like a steeplechase. In their time, George Washington and Thomas Jefferson enjoyed the races, and the tradition continues today on the first Sunday in May at Winterthur.

The appearance at the Winterthur races of one Valley resident, George "Frolic" Weymouth, has itself become a tradition. Each year Mr. Weymouth coordinates and —in his antique three-quarter-size Park Drag Brewster—leads a parade of as many as fifty horse-drawn gigs, phaetons, carts, traps, surreys, coaches, and wagons as part of race day festivities. An acclaimed painter, collector, and chairman of the board of the Brandywine Conservancy, Mr. Weymouth has turned his home, Big Bend, into a showplace of early-American decorative arts. He is also an avid coachman, one who can plan an elegant picnic at the races as well as drive the coach and four to get there.

In this picnic menu Mr. Weymouth combines the everyday with the elegant, raising ordinary foods to glamorous heights. A hoagie fit for a king is made with caviar and chopped egg on toasted French bread and served on a bed of ice. Even the Caramel Apple attains new stature as the dessert of this festive alfresco meal.

Mr. Weymouth's picnic deserves an extraordinary setting, and the Winterthur estate qualifies handsomely. A glass of chilled vodka, a sunny afternoon, and a wide-open road complete the requirements for a successful picnic on race day.

Menu

Vichyssoise

Caviar Hoagies

Herb Tomatoes ‡

Asparagus Vinaigrette ‡

Caramel Apples

Cookies

Iced Vodka

‡ (recipe not included)

PREPARATION TIPS: CAVIAR

Caviar is one of the world's luxury foods. The most prized caviar is sturgeon roe, although the roe of several other fish is also eaten. One of the best known and most rare is beluga, a Russian caviar with exceptionally large, gray eggs. Sevruga caviar, from the Caspian Sea, is more readily available. It is black, with smaller eggs than beluga, although it too comes from sturgeon.

Red caviar is often salmon roe, and it is widely available in the United States. Its flavor is fishier than that of gray or black caviar. Also popular in the United States is lumpfish caviar from the North Atlantic.

Caviar should always be served chilled. If it must remain on a serving table, caviar should be presented in a bowl nestled in a bed of ice. Dry toast points or dark bread is the usual companion to caviar, as well as lemon wedges. Some people also serve chopped egg as an accompaniment.

The traditional and most suitable drink to serve with caviar is vodka that has been well chilled in the freezer. Also appropriate is dry champagne, well chilled.

VICHYSSOISE

Number of Servings: 8

Preparation Time: 20 minutes

Cooking Time: 30 minutes

INGREDIENTS:

8 large potatoes, peeled and sliced
2 leeks, peeled and sliced
6 stalks celery, sliced
6 large onions, peeled and sliced
2 cups water
1 teaspoon salt
1 teaspoon cayenne pepper
3 cups chicken stock
4 cups light cream
4 tablespoons chives, finely chopped

DIRECTIONS:

Put potatoes, leeks, celery, and onions into a pan with the water, salt, and pepper. Cover pan and cook very slowly until vegetables become quite mushy. Stir in stock over the heat until soup comes to a boil. Cool, and rub through a coarse strainer. Chill in refrigerator until ice-cold, add cream, and garnish with chives. Serve in individual bowls surrounded by crushed ice.

CAVIAR HOAGIES

Number of Servings: 8

Preparation Time: 15 minutes

Cooking Time: 15 minutes

INGREDIENTS:

4 loaves French bread (baguette type)
1 stick butter
8 ounces sour cream
12 eggs, hard-boiled
12 ounces black caviar
12 ounces red caviar
2 onions, chopped

DIRECTIONS:

Slice bread in half lengthwise. Hollow halves out, spread with butter, and toast. Cut each half in half, for 16 pieces of toasted bread. Spread each piece with sour cream. Remove the egg yolks and crumble them. On each piece of toast, place a stripe of yolk lengthwise down the center; add a black caviar stripe on one side of the yolk, and a red caviar stripe on the other side. Garnish with chopped onions and a dollop of sour cream. Serve on a bed of ice covered with lettuce.

CARAMEL APPLES

Number of Servings: 8	
Preparation Time: 20 minutes	
Cooking Time: 30 minutes	

INGREDIENTS:

2 cups sugar
1 cup light corn syrup
1½ cups heavy cream
½ cup water
¼ cup butter
½ teaspoon salt
1 teaspoon vanilla
8 large apples (red delicious are good)
12 sticks
2 cups nuts, crushed

DIRECTIONS:

Cook sugar, corn syrup, 1 cup cream, and ¼ cup water in a heavy saucepan for about 10 minutes. Add the rest of the cream and water and continue cooking for about 5 minutes. Add butter, a little at a time, until a candy thermometer reaches 230 degrees; lower the heat and cook until the thermometer reaches 245 degrees. (The syrup forms a ball when dropped into cold water.) Let stand for 10 minutes and then add salt and vanilla.

Push stick into the end of each apple. Dip apple into the caramel mixture, roll apple in crushed nuts, and place it on wax paper.

THE GOLFERS' LUNCHEON WITH ARNOLD AND WINNIE PALMER

Casual entertaining suits Arnold and Winnie Palmer to a tee. One of the world's golfing legends and a force on the Professional Golf Association's senior tour, Arnold Palmer, also a committed businessman, occasionally finds his life reaching a frantic pace. Often his luncheons combine business with pleasure. For the Palmers, whether it is on the links at Latrobe, Pennsylvania, or overlooking a fairway in Florida, there is no better place to hold a luncheon than at a golf course.

This outdoor golfers' luncheon has a decidedly Hawaiian flair. It includes an Oahu Salad of shellfish, fresh fruit, and tangy onion accented by Celery Seed Dressing. Hawaiian Meatballs, topped with a sweet-and-sour sauce, are accompanied by Macadamia Nut Cake. A dessert of fresh fruit becomes a touch exotic when served in a hollowed-out pineapple half.

Hand-blown blue glass dishware graces the luncheon table, creating a stained-glass effect on the cloth beneath. The centerpiece, an oversized compote, holds a whimsical arrangement of Hawaiian orchids and golf balls. Bamboo mats evoke images of the Orient, as do the exotically patterned napkins.

Business associates and friends alike will revel in the chance to spend noontime out of doors, eating a relaxed meal, even if they are not overlooking the fourth hole! Be sure to have plenty of minted iced tea on hand to cool midafternoon thirsts. A light white wine, such as a Johannisberg Riesling, also makes a nice companion for this meal.

Menu

Oahu Salad with Celery Seed Dressing

Hawaiian Meatballs

Brown Rice ‡

Fruit Platter ‡

Banana-Macadamia Nut Cake

Lemonade

Iced tea

‡ (recipe not included)

The Wilmington Country Club plays host to many avid golfers, Arnold Palmer among them. The luncheon table is located so that Mr. Palmer and his guests can observe the fourth hole.

The table is set with cobalt-blue glass designs of the eighteenth century. The plates and double-lipped pitcher are hand blown, a hint of traditional craft in today's living. The glass centerpiece displays a lovely Phaleonopsis orchid. It is held in place by Spanish moss and golf balls.

Other objects include modern aqua-colored glasses, and silver from Reed & Barton.

Preparation Tips: Fresh Fruit Desserts

On a hot summer's afternoon there is nothing quite as refreshing as a chilled fruit dessert. Whether offered as a whole fruit or in a salad, fruit desserts are light and refreshing, and—for the host and hostess—easy.

Be daring and try unfamiliar fruits, such as the many tropical fruits that are now coming onto the American market. Papayas, mangos, and kiwis are by now familiar sights in the produce section. Carambolas (sometimes known as "star fruit"), cherimoyas, litchis, and loquats, among others, are becoming more readily available and offer wonderful tastes and uses to be explored.

Fruit that is picked before it is completely ripe can be ripened quite easily. One method is to place it in a partially closed paper bag at room temperature until it ripens. Another is to wrap fruit loosely, and individually, in paper towels and let it ripen in a bowl or a basket at room temperature. Either way, check the fruit frequently, and refrigerate as soon as it is ripe.

Wash and dry all fruit before it is served. Although washing does not remove all traces of the chemicals used in the fruit's cultivation, it will remove the most harmful bacteria, chemicals, and dirt. Do not soak fruit, since it loses its flavor very quickly when immersed in water.

Fresh fruit is lovely served alone or with light cream and sugar. It also lends itself well to being marinated in any number of liqueurs. Some frequently suggested combinations are peaches, plums, and cherries in brandy; strawberries in Grand Marnier or rum; melons in port or Midori; raspberries in kirsch; apricots in amaretto; oranges in brandy or Cointreau. Liqueur-soaked fruits can be served chilled or flambéed, the fruit at room temperature and the liqueur slightly warmed for easy ignition.

Oahu Salad with Celery Seed Dressing

Number of Servings: 6

Preparation Time: 30 minutes

Cooking Time: 2 minutes

INGREDIENTS:

1 pound shrimp
2–3 grapefruits
4–5 navel oranges
1 large Spanish onion, sliced
2 avocados
Leaf lettuce
Celery Seed Dressing

DIRECTIONS:

Cook shrimp in boiling water for 2 minutes; plunge into cold water. Shell shrimp, leaving tails on. Cut grapefruits in half and remove sections. Place in large mixing bowl. Peel oranges and divide into sections, leaving membranes on; add to grapefruit. Add onion and shrimp to fruit. Prior to serving, slice avocados and toss with other ingredients. Serve on lettuce and dress with Celery Seed Dressing.

✣

Celery Seed Dressing

Yield: 1 ½ cups

Preparation Time: 10 minutes

INGREDIENTS:

⅓ cup sugar
1 teaspoon dry mustard
1 teaspoon salt
1 small onion, minced
⅓ cup white vinegar
1 cup oil
1 tablespoon celery seed

DIRECTIONS:

Add first 4 ingredients to blender or small mixing bowl. Slowly add part of vinegar, blending or mixing at medium speed. Add the rest of the vinegar and oil, beating until creamy. Add celery seed.

✣

HAWAIIAN MEATBALLS

Number of Servings: 6 portions

Preparation Time: 35 minutes

Cooking Time: 30 minutes (total for meatballs and sauce)

INGREDIENTS:

Meatballs
1½ pounds ground beef
⅔ cup cracker crumbs
½ cup onion, chopped
⅔ cup evaporated milk
1 teaspoon seasoned salt
⅓ cup flour
3 tablespoons shortening

Sweet and Sour Sauce
1 13½-ounce can pineapple chunks
2 tablespoons cornstarch
½ cup vinegar
½ cup brown sugar
2 tablespoons soy sauce
2 tablespoons lemon juice

1 cup green pepper, coarsely chopped
1 tablespoon pimento, chopped

DIRECTIONS:

Meatballs—Combine first 5 ingredients; mix lightly but thoroughly. Shape meat mixture into 30 meatballs. Roll each in flour. Brown meatballs in shortening. Drain excess fat. Meanwhile, prepare Sweet and Sour Sauce. Pour over meatballs. Simmer, covered, for 15 minutes.

Sweet and Sour Sauce—Drain pineapple chunks; reserve pineapple. Measure syrup. Add water to make 1 cup. Blend together pineapple syrup and cornstarch until smooth. Stir in next 4 ingredients. Cook until thickened and clear. Add pineapple, green pepper, and pimento; mix well. Cover. Simmer over low heat for 15 minutes.

BANANA-MACADAMIA NUT CAKE

Yield: 1 cake

Preparation Time: 25 minutes

Cooking Time: 40 minutes

INGREDIENTS:

1 stick butter
1 cup sugar
2 eggs
2 cups flour

2 teaspoons baking powder
1 teaspoon baking soda
½ teaspoon salt
½ cup milk

½ teaspoon cinnamon
½ teaspoon ginger
Pinch of cloves
½ cup golden raisins
½ cup macadamia nuts, slivered or chopped, reserving
    ¼ cup
½ cup shredded coconut
1 ½ cups mashed bananas

DIRECTIONS:

Cream the butter and sugar in medium-sized mixing bowl. Add eggs. In a smaller bowl sift together flour, baking powder, baking soda, and salt. Add to butter mixture, small portions at a time. Add milk. Blend thoroughly. Add spices, raisins, nuts, coconut, and mashed bananas. Mix well. Place the ¼ cup of reserved nuts in the bottom of a prepared bundt pan. Pour the batter into it and bake for 40 minutes at 350 degrees. Cool and invert onto serving dish.

A PICNIC BEFORE HOT-AIR BALLOONING WITH GEORGE PLIMPTON

A picnic with George Plimpton could never be ordinary. The author, adventurer, and Renaissance man has played professional football and performed with a circus—just for the experience. He is a lover of fireworks, a hater of airborne model airplanes, and a demon tennis player. He is also a collector. With his wife, Freddy, Mr. Plimpton collects anything having to do with birds, shells, and butterflies, be it a ceramic piece of folk art or a print. Mr. Plimpton also collects anecdotes about famous literary, political, and artistic friends and neighbors, including Truman Capote, Kurt Vonnegut, and *New Yorker* cartoonist Charles Addams.

With his wealth of experience and diversity of interest, Mr. Plimpton is bound to make picnicking a unique experience. Lunch will have to provide enough energy to fuel the balloonists. The solution? A New England clam bake, full of high-protein seafood, filling but not heavy, and special enough to precede the memorable afternoon's entertainment. Four people in the balloon plus two people to ride in the "chase car" make six the perfect number for this hot-air experience.

New England clam chowder, steamed clams, and grilled lobster are the focus of the meal, which is accompanied by grill-baked potatoes and steamed corn on the cob. So that the balloon can get off the ground, save the luscious Apricot Brandy Cake until after touch-down.

Serve a chilled chardonnay or a regional New England beer, for those who prefer. Native New England cranberry juice with just a touch of sparkling water makes a fine nonalcoholic alternative.

Menu

New England Clam Chowder

Steamed Clams with Butter

Corn on the Cob

Grilled Lobster

Grill-Baked Potatoes

Apricot Brandy Cake

Beer

Iced Tea

The open stretch of lawn surrounding the back pond at Winterthur Gardens is the site for the landing of a colorful hot-air balloon. A picnic lunch awaits the hungry fliers. Elegance is added to the country setting by Winterthur reproduction "Torquay" earthenware, made by Mottahedeh, based on the shell motif of an English Staffordshire plate, ca. 1820, in the Winterthur Collection. The shell motif is very appropriate to a feast of foods from the sea. The deep blue of the design adds another dimension to the predominately red, brown, and gold hues of the table. Winterthur reproduction silverware by Reed & Barton, sporting a shell pattern on the handles, continues the sea theme.
Other items shown include a modern glass pitcher and modern glass pilsners.

If something can be forgotten for a picnic, it will be. But for a special meal, careful preparation is always necessary; and a picnic is no exception.

Make a list of the basics needed: glasses, plates, cutlery, napkins, corkscrew, bottle opener, salt, pepper, and so on. Then go through the menu and add the unusual items needed: hibachi for grilling lobster (if a pit is not to be used), a small fondue pot (perhaps one normally used for chocolate fondue) for melting butter, a large pot for steaming clams, a pot for heating chowder, bowls and soup spoons, clam picks, and so forth. Assemble everything beforehand and check items off the list. Then review the menu and make sure you have not forgotten anything!

Several companies make easily portable collapsible tables, perfect for toting in the trunk of a car. With the addition of folding chairs, it is possible to create virtually an entire dining room on a hillside. Nice extra touches include seat cushions for the folding chairs and a tablecloth for the table.

Flowers are a nice touch and can be transported in a cooler along with soft drinks and perishables. Be sure to place them on top with plenty of space between them and the lid so that they do not get crushed.

Once at the picnic, use an appropriate container for the centerpiece. If crystal and china are the order of the day, bring along a fairly formal vase. If the meal is more casual, a bright ceramic pitcher, a decorative wine bottle, or even a hollowed-out pumpkin or a large squash makes a relaxed and informal centerpiece.

It is essential that perishable foods be kept chilled. Too often at picnics foods are left out in the heat and sun under the assumption that they will be eaten quickly. Seafood, especially, spoils quickly and with very unpleasant consequences. Bring extra coolers if necessary so that there is plenty of storage space for drinks and food. And if food looks or smells bad, discard it immediately. Do not take chances by eating it!

NEW ENGLAND CLAM CHOWDER

Number of Servings: 6

Preparation Time: 25 minutes

INGREDIENTS:

3 slices salt pork, chopped
2 cups water
4 medium potatoes, peeled and diced
½ cup onion, chopped
1 pint shucked clams, chopped

2 cups milk
1 cup light cream
3 tablespoons flour
3 tablespoons butter
Salt
Pepper
Parsley

DIRECTIONS:

In a large saucepan fry salt pork until crisp, add 2 cups water, diced potatoes, and onion. Cook covered for about 15 minutes, or until potatoes are tender. Stir in clams, 1½ cups milk, and cream. Blend remaining ½ cup milk with flour; stir into the chowder. Cook until bubbly, add butter, and cook 1 minute more. Salt and pepper to taste. Garnish with parsley.

STEAMED CLAMS WITH BUTTER

Number of Servings: 6

Preparation Time: 15 minutes

Cooking Time: 20 minutes

INGREDIENTS:

> 6 dozen littleneck clams in the shell
> 9 gallons cold water
> 3 cups salt
> 3 tablespoons cornmeal
> 6 clam nets
> 4 cups hot water
> 1 pound butter, melted

DIRECTIONS:

Wash clams thoroughly. In a large kettle, combine 3 gallons of cold water and 1 cup of salt. Place clams in the salt water and let stand for 15 minutes. Rinse well. Repeat the salt water soak twice more, and on the last soak add the 3 tablespoons of cornmeal to the water. Rinse well. Place 1 dozen clams in each clam net and secure.

Place nets with clams on a rack in a large kettle holding the 4 cups of hot water. Cover tightly and steam for 20 minutes or until shells open. Discard any clams that do not open.

Melt butter and divide into 6 portions. Serve with steamed clams.

CORN ON THE COB

Number of Servings: 6

Preparation Time: 10 minutes

Cooking Time: 30 minutes

INGREDIENTS:

> 6 fresh ears of corn
> ¼ pound butter
> Salt
> Pepper

DIRECTIONS:

Husk corn, remove all silk, and wash in cold water. Spread ears of corn with butter. Salt and pepper to taste. Wrap each ear of corn with foil and place on the grill and cover. Bake for about 30 minutes (turning several times) until tender.

GRILLED LOBSTER

Number of Servings: 6
Preparation Time: 10 minutes
Cooking Time: 20 minutes

INGREDIENTS:

> 6 lobsters (1–1¼ pounds each)
> 1 cup butter
> Lemon wedges

DIRECTIONS:

Have the fish market kill the lobsters by severing their spinal cords. Split each lobster lengthwise, so it will not curl on the grill.

Melt butter in a bowl of hot water. Once the butter is melted, leave it to cool. Soon you will see a whitish sediment at the bottom of the bowl. Pour the melted butter carefully into another container, leaving the sediment behind. Discard the sediment.

Heat the grill. Arrange the lobsters cut side up in a shallow baking pan and brush with the clarified butter. Cover, and grill for 20 minutes, brushing with more butter from time to time.

Serve with lemon wedges and nutcrackers.

GRILL-BAKED POTATOES

Number of Servings: 6
Preparation Time: 10 minutes
Cooking Time: 1 hour

INGREDIENTS:

> 6 medium-sized baking potatoes
> 6 tablespoons butter
> Salt
> Pepper

DIRECTIONS:

Cut wedge out of each potato approximately 2 inches long and 1 inch wide. Insert 1 tablespoon of butter and salt and pepper. Wrap potato in foil, keeping cut section on top, and place on the grill. Cover and bake for 1 hour.

APRICOT BRANDY CAKE

Number of Servings: 10

Preparation Time: 10 minutes

Cooking Time: 1 hour, 15 minutes

INGREDIENTS:

3 cups sugar
1 cup butter
6 eggs
3 cups flour
¼ teaspoon baking powder
½ teaspoon salt
1 cup sour cream
1 tablespoon rum extract
1 tablespoon lemon extract
1 tablespoon orange extract
½ cup apricot brandy + 3 tablespoons
1 tablespoon vanilla extract
Confectioners' sugar

DIRECTIONS:

Cream sugar and butter together. Add eggs one at a time and beat until light and fluffy. Sift dry ingredients together; add to butter mixture. Mix in sour cream. Beat well. Mix extracts and ½ cup brandy together. Add to batter and mix.

Bake at 350 degrees for 1 hour, 15 minutes, in a 10-inch buttered and floured tube pan. Cool cake and remove from pan. Dust with confectioners' sugar and drizzle with 3 tablespoons of apricot brandy.

Store in a cool place.

PETE AND ELISE DU PONT'S PICNIC IN THE AZALEA WOODS

The Azalea Woods at Winterthur were one of Henry Francis du Pont's passions, designed to have a surprise around each bend in the path. Subtle combinations of hues ranging from vivid crimson and salmon to delicate lavender and white grace the naturalized woodlands during the azaleas' height of bloom in May and early June. At each turn, a dramatic vista, vibrant shrub, or intimate glen delights the visitor.

How appropriate that the du Ponts of today, the former governor of Delaware Pierre Samuel du Pont and his wife Elise, chose these woods to display their picnic in celebration of spring. A simple but splendid luncheon, with a few surprises of its own, suits perfectly the lush, alfresco setting.

Cold Roast Quail, Grilled Baby Lamb Chops, and Homemade Watercress Mayonnaise highlight the sumptuous meal. But wait! Rounding out the menu are plain, sliced fresh Tomatoes, sliced hard Salami, unadorned fresh Homemade Bread, and even Peanut Butter and Jelly Sandwiches. The common thread? Everything is fresh, delicious, and elegantly presented.

Simple and dignified, but with a few unexpected features, the setting displays a mix of the elegant and the everyday similar to the menu's. Snowy white linen reflects sunlight onto sterling flatware and crystal. But sitting in the midst of this splendor is an ordinary cardboard egg carton—a humorous touch and the most appropriate container for sinfully rich Rum-Laced Hard-Boiled Eggs.

The transportation to this afternoon affair is a Dual Cowl Phaeton Model H, introduced at the 1931 auto show in New York. Its maker? E. Paul du Pont, another of the family's innovators, who gave the car its unique Lalique hood ornament and "dP" insignia to set it apart from all the rest.

Reproduction porcelain in the "Winterthur" pattern, from an early nineteenth-century French dinner service made by Jacques Jugeat, is combined with a Winterthur reproduction eighteenth-century brass monteith used for chilling wine bottles and glasses. Winterthur's reproduction eighteenth-century "Ch'ien Lung," by Strohein & Romann, is perfect for the napkins used in this elegant picnic setting.
Other items shown include Winterthur reproduction silverware from Reed & Barton and Winterthur's reproduction nineteenth-century stemware.

Menu

Stuffed Hard-Boiled Eggs Laced with Rum

Cold Roast Quail

Cold Grilled Baby Lamb Chops

Peanut Butter and Jelly Sandwiches

Deli Platter

American Goat Cheese Round

Genoa Salami

Beefsteak Tomatoes

Homemade Watercress Mayonnaise

Homemade Whole Wheat Bread

Grapes

Linzer Torte

Red Zinger Iced Tea

California Heitz Cabernet Sauvignon

California Pinot Noir, Edna Valley 1981

Homemade mayonnaise is without compare. It is so much richer, smoother, and more flavorful than "store-bought" that—once tried—it is impossible to go back to the commercial product. Homemade mayonnaise is very high in fat, in cholesterol, and in calories; eating it is worth every twinge of guilt.

Mayonnaise can be made easily by hand or in a blender or food processor. No matter which of these methods is used, the trick to smooth mayonnaise is to beat the mixture continuously and add the oil very slowly, allowing the mayonnaise to thicken.

Watercress is only one of any number of potential flavors—the choice is limited only by the taste buds and the imagination. Many standard salad dressings begin with mayonnaise, including Russian, Thousand Island, green goddess, ranch, and creamy Italian.

Try mixing into mayonnaise fresh herbs like parsley, dill, basil, coriander, chives, or tarragon, or spices like chili powder, curry powder, or paprika, before using mayonnaise on sandwiches or in salads. Prepared mustards, horseradish, fruit and vegetable chutneys, and sauces like Worcestershire or soy also add interest.

Just remember, eaten in moderation, mayonnaise is no worse for the figure than . . . chocolate cake!

STUFFED HARD-BOILED EGGS LACED WITH RUM

Yield: 1 dozen eggs

Preparation Time: 20 minutes

INGREDIENTS:

12 eggs, hard-boiled and shelled
½ cup homemade watercress mayonnaise
Lettuce or fresh parsley for garnish
2 tablespoons rum

DIRECTIONS:

Cut top from each egg, one-third the way down. Scoop out yolk and place in a medium-size mixing bowl. Mix mayonnaise and yolks together and, using a pastry bag, pipe mixture into the egg halves. Place stuffed eggs back into the egg carton lined with lettuce or fresh parsley. The egg carton is the serving dish. Lace stuffed eggs with rum.

COLD ROAST QUAIL

Number of Servings: 8

Preparation Time: 10 minutes, plus thawing time

Cooking Time: 60 minutes

INGREDIENTS:

8 quail (if frozen, thaw to room temperature)
Salt and pepper
4–6 tablespoons butter
8 slices bacon

DIRECTIONS:

Rinse birds in cold water. Pat dry. Sprinkle with salt and pepper inside and out. Melt butter and baste. Lay bacon over breast. Roast loosely covered in foil. Uncover the quail the last 20 minutes. Bake at 375 degrees for 1 hour or until golden brown. Cool completely before serving.

COLD GRILLED BABY LAMB CHOPS

Number of Servings: 8–16 chops

Preparation Time: 10 minutes, plus 3 hours marinating time

Cooking Time: 25–30 minutes

INGREDIENTS:

½ cup vinegar
¼ cup water
⅛–¼ teaspoon ground cloves
⅛–¼ teaspoon ground cinnamon
Pepper, freshly cracked
¼ cup red wine
8–16 baby lamb chops

DIRECTIONS:

Bring the vinegar, water, cloves, cinnamon, and pepper to a boil, let it cool, and add ¼ cup red wine. Pour the mixture over the lamp chops and let them marinate for 3 hours at room temperature. Drain marinade from lamb chops and place chops on a hot grill for 25 to 30 minutes. Cool chops and store in refrigerator until ready to serve.

HOMEMADE WATERCRESS MAYONNAISE

Yield: 1 cup

Preparation Time: 25 minutes

INGREDIENTS:

2 egg yolks, at room temperature
1 tablespoon prepared mustard
2 cups peanut oil
2 tablespoons lemon juice
¾ cup watercress leaves

DIRECTIONS:

In the bowl of a food processor, place the egg yolks and mustard. Turn on the machine and begin to add the oil, very slowly at first. As soon as the sauce begins to thicken and become smooth, the oil may be added more rapidly. While the machine is running, add the lemon juice and chopped watercress until a smooth consistency is achieved.

LINZER TORTE

Number of Servings: 6–8

Preparation Time: 30 minutes

Cooking Time: 40–50 minutes

INGREDIENTS:

1 ½ cups sifted flour
¼ teaspoon salt
1 cup sugar
1 cup butter
Rind from 1 lemon, grated
3 egg yolks
1 cup unblanched almonds, ground
½ teaspoon cinnamon, ground
¼ teaspoon cloves, ground
8 ounces cherry jam
Confectioners' sugar

DIRECTIONS:

In small mixing bowl sift flour with salt. Set aside. Cream sugar with butter until mixture is light and fluffy. Add lemon rind and the egg yolks, one at a time, beating well after each addition. Gradually add the flour to the creamed mixture, alternating with the ground almonds, which have already been mixed with the cinnamon and cloves. Chill the dough.

Roll out enough dough to cover the bottom of a springform pan or flan ring. Layer should be about 2 inches thick. Make a rim ¼ inch thick to reach about 1 ½ inches up the sides of the form. Spread the dough with the jam. Roll the remaining dough into strips and form a lattice over the jam. Bake the torte in a moderately hot oven (375 degrees) for 40 to 50 minutes, or until it is lightly browned on top. Remove the cooled torte from the pan, fill the holes on top with more jam, and sprinkle with confectioners' sugar.

Index

Note: *Italic* page numbers refer to captions and illustrations.

242